To Kathie,
with love,
Bette

The
THUNDER
of
DEEP THOUGHT

"HOUSE OF THE SUN NOTEBOOKS," NUMBER TWO

HUANG XIANG

Translated by Teresa Zimmerman-Liu

A SAMPSONIA WAY™ PUBLICATION I SAMPSONIAWAY.ORG
IMPRINT OF CITY OF ASYLUM

The Thunder of Deep Thought —
"House of the Sun Notebooks," Number Two. ©2014 by Huang Xiang
Published in the United States.
Translation © Teresa Zimmerman-Liu, 2014

All Rights Reserved

Published by Sampsonia Way,
the publishing arm of City of Asylum
330 Sampsonia Way
Pittsburgh, Pennsylvania 15212-4440

www.sampsoniaway.org
www.cityofasylumpittsburgh.org

All facts and characters appearing in this work are fictitious.
Any resemblance to real persons, living or dead,
is purely coincidental.

Sampsonia Way Managing Editor: Silvia Duarte
Book design: Michael Solano-Mullings
Cover artwork: Huang Xiang
Cover design: Michael Solano-Mullings

COVER TEXT TRANSLATION

Ice Blue Poetry

In the days before it was covered with ice and snow and after it was covered with ice and snow and while it is covered with ice and snow or while the ice and snow are melting due to climate change, it has always remained the same planet, hanging and turning in time and space, the same great Earth under the same orb of the sun, where humanity has lived or is living, and from which humanity will disappear in the end.

In the time and space apart from time and space, who were the earliest visitors to the ice blue world? Who can interpret the mysterious meaning of the ice and snow? Who has discovered the inexplicable, hidden secrets of civilization under the vast layers of ice? I believe that the past, present, and future of different times and spaces are all the same moment of now. The earth and sun both belong to the ultimate meaning of the same ball of ice.

—Translated by Teresa Zimmerman-Liu

Dedicated to Irene Vongher Vincent

Contents

Notes Left On Celestial Bodies	13
The Thinking Soul (Fragments)	49
The Waterfall Of The Human Body	93
Six Topics On Poetics	101
The Thunder Of Deep Thought	121
Emotional Philosophy --Modern "Poetics" I	123
The Sun of Flesh --Modern "Poetics" II	133
Heidegger in a "Pot" --Modern "Poetics" III	135
Understanding the Depths of the Human Body: Universal Emotions --Modern "Poetics" IV	184
Translating Silence --Modern "Poetics" V	192
The Origins Of The Universe	199
The "Present" Abyss	201
Ancient Facula	205
The Vast Darkness of "Death"	209
"Humanity" is Formed in the Attempting	214
The Darkness that Illuminates itself with a Candle	218
The Riddle of Essence	221
The Empty Cave of the "Non-existent" Body	226
The Mother of the Universe	229
The "Image" of the Imageless World	232
About the Author	239

The **THUNDER** *of* **DEEP THOUGHT**

"HOUSE OF THE SUN NOTEBOOKS," NUMBER TWO

Notes Left on Celestial Bodies

—Universal Emotions
(1968-1969)

PREFACE

1

Some people are martyrs for religion, martyrs for beliefs; I am a martyr for poetry.

2

When people marvel at the rich imagination in poetry,
Poetry marvels even more at its own poverty.

3

I flit back and forth between past and present, giving a monologue between life and death; my thoughts are like a ray of soft light.

4

I appear in the world for as many years as poetry appears in the world.
The way of poetry is not just a path for my feet to walk on, but also a trail through which my head must bushwhack.
The smooth surface of the path is paved, not with rough cobblestones, but with the broken pieces of my skull as I shout through endless centuries.

1

A two-legged beast under the countless stars in the sky asks: "Who am I?"

2
What is the world that stretches forth outside of me?
What am I when living, and what am I when dead?
------------------When I demand the answers of myself,
I do not believe my own cerebral, neural, and ocular systems…

3
I finally found the door to the universe:
I shook it a little ------------------ a meteor fell; it was the starry brass hinge
falling from that door. I discovered that I had died there long ago.

4
The poet asked the philosopher:
Do you think the great and small celestial bodies up in the heavens move along the orbits of your philosophy?

5
My form is natural, and I am formed by Nature.

6
From outside my body, I saw the image of a picture of my own heart;
I opened up the pictures of my inner heart to all kinds of outward forms.

7
The beauty of Nature endows me with emotions.

8
"Putting into practice" is the marriage of my fumbling in the darkness with my inner light.

9
Because my thoughts became orderly,
I thought I had discovered the order of the natural world.

10
That night, the world answered my startled, doubting gaze, saying:
"I am you."

11
I continue living,
as my thoughts defeat the shell of my fleshly body in debate.

12
Faith is a human construction; after a long period of time,
The houses for these concepts will collapse.

13
Is there anything that can be trusted?
When I escape from the nets of human concepts, all philosophies are shattered.

14
Have you discovered anything? Nothing at all. ---------------------
Although from the regular patterns on the body of a viper, I discovered things that we say in chemistry, biology, and physiology are governed by natural laws.

15
Because they were included in my sight, all the flowers were given different shapes and colors, and they were also named; Because they were included in my hearing, the bees took away a buzzing sound, and this buzz was given a different meaning from the sound of the ocean's waves.

16
What I apprehend of all things
Is not the entire meaning of air, water, or light;
That which is included in my voice,
Is not entirely blended with the languages of insects, birds, and beasts.

17
Green grass encompasses milk;
Milk encompasses spiritual knowledge.

18
My senses produce sensations, and the latter are surprised at the mysteriousness of the former.

19
Thoughts are formed from sensations and are solidified in written words; clear and lucid concepts have appeared. Going from sensory to extra-sensory causes the existence of doubts about one's senses.

20
When my consciousness dies, written words, I no longer recognize it.

21
The spread of freedom begins with the space to explore one's heart.

22
I thought that what I knew was because I relied upon that knowledge; it was because that knowledge matched my personal needs.

23
I gave my pictures to the outside world; I am a collector, an exhibitor, who hoards countless pictures; I am a miracle that produces billions of artistic pictures.

24
Materialism is assured of the existence of physical matter; Materialism is frightened and awed by spiritual gifts.

25
Materialism fought with idealism, and the two evenly divided the inheritance of wisdom, but the eclectics try to possess it all for themselves.

26
Philosophy uses reason to dissect the world;
Poetics uses emotion to explain the world.

27
Reason is the tailor who clothes all kinds of religious tenets, theories, and thoughts, cutting and stitching them into eternally unchanging rituals.

28
Reason thought itself absolutely perfect, so it cut off its wings of lively speculation and quietly settled down into the nest of truth.

29
When reason spun its web in an attempt to entrap the world, it only caught a leaf, a fly, and a drop of dew.

30
The wheels on a car do not understand, nor do they wish to understand, why they spin.

31
The mountain top covered in snow makes no sound because it is tired of hearing the loud cries from the grassy plain at its foot.

32
The stars bend down to listen to the arguments of human thought across the ages,
And with humor they wink their eyes.

33
The universe in its essence is a heavenly letter without words, a scroll rolled out in its vastness; over the past thousand years humans have only deciphered a few phrases.

34
"Oh life, come back here!" ---One night I startled myself screaming in my dreams, and when I awoke I fell into a dark abyss.

35
The eyes of a blind man cannot see, and he thinks that the sunlight has been exhausted.

36
The dead got no results from their arguing, but the living continue to argue ceaselessly.

37
They use sharp knives in their debates thinking that words are not as sharp as knife blades.

38
One day a voice issued out of the depths of the darkness saying: "Run quickly, there are people coming after you."

39
Freedom was jostled and shoved in a pile of humanity, crushed until it could not catch its breath;
It returned to Nature and felt that it could breathe freely once more.

40
When I trace the meaning of "humanity" back to a pile of flesh, I am always surprised at the marvelous continuance and resurrection of this flesh across time never-ending.
This flesh exists in sensation and thought; before "death," this flesh moved on the face of the earth.
Thus, I realize that I am my "lie."

41
Because of my habits I think I am clear about what I am doing; when I do not trust my habits, I discover that what I do is not self-aware, and I do not know what I am doing or why I am doing it.

42
What has been left on the surface of the earth? Nothing at all; all things that have happened are those which have not yet happened.

43
Desires bound me to the cross of life;
Death came along and loosened the bonds.

44
Life is the face of death,
And death is the shape of life.

45
My life continued my life,
My death continued my death.

46
My life and death began at the same moment.
When I wanted to die, I had already begun to live there.

47
"One day in heaven is the same as one year among humans."
This is the great imagination of my ancestors.

Among their skeletons, rotting like a dung heap, I dug out golden nuggets of wisdom! "The fastest spreads out in the midst of the slowest."

48
I felt alone among a group of strangers. My body crawled upon "reality"; my spirit was in another place.

1
Return my naked men,
Return my naked women,
Return my naked universe.

2
Male and female belong to the naked wind, water, atmosphere and earth;
They are the moving world and the world's movement.

3
Is there anything in the essence of Nature that is worth it for us to conceal?

4
If we do not marvel that sex is a biological and physiological mystery,
Then who are we to understand enthusiasm, aspiration, impetuosity, and desire?

5
That which tempts me is the vigorous craving for life.

6
Morality is the reaction to lust.

7
Seek to escape the slavery of morally following the law!

8
Surplus desires are the portrait of health.

9
A family is just such a construction—
It joins a man and a woman, and then they both hold tight to the latch-key of the other's spirit.

10
It is the momentary rush of emotions,
It is the temptation of mutual trust,
It is a kind of restless surprise and delight,
It is the submission to mutual self-forgetting.

11
Do not hide your love in the shadows,
It is healthier to let the sun shine upon it.

12
I am satisfied with myself; I am not ashamed;
------Because I am not so shameless as to hide my loves and desires.

13
Love is the discovery and digging out of the beloved; it fails when one tires of this.

14
He who loves a woman purely,
First loves that she is a person.

15
A jealous heart is like a cuckolded husband—
Both his arms are folded tightly across his chest,
His chin is trembling, his facial expression is cold,
And he is always waiting for the chance to take revenge.

16
The cracks around the door of jealousy shoot out bright rays of love's light when you jiggle the door.

17
The crafty businessman takes what he demands from art,
And then he thinks that art has cheated him.

18
Government realizes the honesty of art and tries to find ways to usurp it.

19
The foot that is planted on someone else's spine
Will always feel a bit unstable.

20
Mute endurance, which does not shout, cries out for sympathy.

21
This is morality------
If love runs out freely like a waterfall,
In waves that fill up countless hearts and spirits.

22
The little tree was jealous of the forest and wanted to soak up all the sunlight for itself, but it forgot that enough sunlight for all the trees would burn him to death.

23
Some people are large rivers, combining countless tributary streams;
Some people are small streams, hiding far away from the large rivers.
When the large rivers flood, they drown out the small streams,
And the bubbles appearing on the water's surface come from the streams under water saying, glug, glug ...

24
Be careful. Don't touch it -------
A wife's self-respect is a wound that is easily infected by dirty things.

25
My eyes always meet these few eyes-----all that is left are eyes filled with desire and curiosity, tired eyes, clean eyes.

26
The concept of good originates in the phenomenon of evil; it is the moral inclination used by human society to ameliorate the psychological relationships between people; it is a hint of the human capacity to hate and fear actions that endanger society and to demand they be controlled.

27
Is there a reliable truth? It is the goal of our tendencies; it is the externalization of our penchant for demanding accurate and practical material forms.

28
So what do we think beauty really is? It plays tricks on us psychologically, calling up our pleasurable emotions; its form is not truer, longer-lasting, or more stable than the forms of changing clouds; it follows society's desires from different eras, but it is not faithful to any one era.

29
Beauty is faithless, just as the floating clouds in the sky have millions of variations and as the bubbles in the ocean turn and disappear in an instant.

30
Thought is as if Nature lent me a mirror, and when I planned to hide my face and mouth, it reflected my true image.

31
I am a rock that is able to think, a maggot that can speak.

32
Strong and weak, rich and poor are the two extremes between which human life and existence vacillate; morality tries to balance them.

33
Civilized society is a garden planned and cultivated by human labor.

34
Capability is selfish. There must be differences. There must be competition. Let peace resolve the conflicts.

35
Power does not see the honor of wisdom and throws it off a high peak into a deep valley.

36
Those who are dignified, upright, and great are the ones who forgive those who do not forgive them.

37
When the flooding mountain stream recedes, a few yellow leaves, floating on the water's surface at the edge of a swirling eddy, imagine that they subdued the violent winds and rushing waters.

38
A pedal-driven water wheel moves in an endless cycle from the beginning around to the beginning again. When I saw the image of the water wheel moving beneath my feet, I thought it had changed, but both my feet were still moving in the same place.

39
The electric light said to light: "Now you have changed; you used to be anemic in an oil lamp."
The light answered it saying: "I am still the same as I was. You have only painted my face with rouge."

40
After the ears of grain are ripe at their "end," they return to their beginning as "seeds."

41
Will I advance? What is the goal? I was walking with both legs moving without beginning or end; the past and the future were both under my feet.

42
The past is without content, the present has no form; everything depends on the presentation.

43
A wave returned the mysteries of the starry sky to me.

44
The future world—freedom and bondage have both been released from their contracts. The boundary between them has disappeared.

45
I arrived at a planet in outer space; it was strewn with the wrecked fossils of cosmic space ships.
Collectively they stood for the centuries through which we have walked and to which we have yet to arrive.

POETRY

A poem is a lion, roaring angrily on the savanna of thought.

1

The name of every great poet is a question mark in the universe.

2

I heard the footsteps of poetry coming forth from the empty ruins of consciousness.

3

Do not look too closely at the sun of poetry, or you will be burned.

4

What the poet gives humanity can be compared to what the sun gives the earth.

5

Poetry is the altar lamp of revolutionary human consciousness, Its light is the nakedness of contemporary forms.

6

A poem is a volume of world history, global history, human history.
All the generations skim through its scroll.

7
Poetry does not follow any society's highest standards and order of thought—
It sees life further and more essentially than logical theories and ethical standards;
It sees Nature materially and blindly turning and moving without any goal;
It sees that love, against the background of the universe, is a man and a woman.

8
Poetry digs out human emotions and measures their depths; it is the highest mark of human consciousness.

9
It is richly expressive art, the flowering of the philosophy of form, the milk of human wisdom.

10
There are seeds of the future here, and only idiots cannot see them.

11
The singer believes completely that the song of the waterfall
Is the explanation of his own spirit.

12
When a small leaf or a tiny piece of gravel is magnified with the lens of the heart to become a feature story, the poet has discovered the unique satisfaction of the world in it.

13
Poems are within the mines and wells of the human spirit,
Steadfastly digging out flames and light.

14
Wise words are laid as bricks to make the poet's eternal tomb.

15
When singers die, their songs cease, too;
The song of poetry never dies.

16
He who takes the bright pearl off the royal crown
Holds out the gem of wisdom to show the world.

17
Cowardly crowds lock up the world in ignorance;
The key of courage opens up all the forbidden places.

18
Go into the kingdom of darkness and light a lamp
Or those who come after you will be terrified.

19
The sky is outside my body;
The pennants are in my heart.

20
Take a step backwards to the abyss of folly;
Take a step forwards to the new precipice.

21
Go into the "unknown" world to discover flowers;
Go into the "known" world to harvest fruit.

22
Poetry is a madman always losing normalcy.

23
It is the Mount Everest of the human spirit.
The air is so thin here, people cannot stand it.
The light is so bright here, it makes people dizzy.
It is so lonely here; there are few human footprints.

24
If in your cerebral cortex the processes of stimulation and repression are balanced, then poems die or are miscarried; if instead of balance there are strong synapses, which affect your psyche and even your physiology and which control all your emotions, pushing your feelings into a state of fullness, then poems will live and slowly put forth their horns, stretching

out their four legs, demanding to be released, and jumping out of your active nerve cells.

25
Most of the life-blood of poetry is gall; this is what gives it its crazy, zealous flavor. There is madness in its eyes: sometimes terror, sometimes worry; sometimes its eyes are perplexed and suffering, and sometimes they are crazy with joy or full of anxiety; sometimes they express the struggle of despair, and sometimes they give glimpses of hope and the courage to fight on.

26
The important things are feelings, imagination, and thought.

27
Paradoxes and great blows are where we see the reality and independence of the world.

28
The broader one's inner sight, the broader the world it encompasses, the deeper the truth it digs out.

29
It is not artistic skill, structural thought, or editing;
Style is original thought and the personality of words.

30
Creativity is not *nouveau riche*;
It is the non-hereditary inheritance and development of poetic capital.

31
It is original, healthy, wild, and fiery.
--This is why it feels that its movement is constricted and that it cannot breathe when you dress it in traditional clothes embroidered with gold thread.
--This is why when a soft hand touches it, the hand feels a sort of carefully polished touch, and the finger will begin to tremble slightly.

32
Go breathe a breath of snow that is wild, cool, warm, and stings the nose. Walk through the forest on a day in early spring, when the snow is just beginning to melt. Go to discover each branch that is putting forth fuzzy new sprouts and feel shivers of pleasure.

33
It is a plowing ox that has put on new bright fur in the new spring;
It is a round spring sun that walks into the shadowy forest and damp mountain valley, tearing down the huge shadows of mountain cliffs;

It is a flock of wild ducks beating their wings on the flowing stream, speaking happily to the women on the banks...

34
This is how your poem becomes a success—
If in the poem the water is flowing, and if the sunlight touches and melts the thin film of ice on a foggy spring day;
If in the poem we can touch the feathers on the flapping wings of the flying birds and the shaking muscles on the backs of the roaring beasts;
If in the poem we can hear the sound of the wind blowing the thick clouds in the skies of the rainy season and the sound of the grass drinking up the dew...
This is how your poem becomes a success.

35
  Yes, poetry is full of the immaterial life of the self-awareness. It understands—
  Those moments of unconscious excitement when you forget yourself in the joy of working;
  The coolness and sweetness of stream water with green leaves floating in it, that we cup up in our hands; the supernatural spirit and tenacity that sunlight gives to sunburned, naked arms;
  The natural marvels in the evening—the sunlight shining on the hills, the fog rising up from the valley floors, the dew already fallen, bringing the cool freshness of dew...

Poetry understands all these things.
It is full of the immaterial life of the self-conscious.

36

Poetry forever walks on the green plains of the life of each age, leaving behind it a trail of green tracks—a miniature of the path of the future.

37

Melt novels, plays, and movies into poetry; make poetry into a form that encompasses them all.

38

Perhaps when poetry struggles to free itself from the shackles of the written word, and seeks to express itself in a wordless form, it will ask for help from sound, color, rhythm, and lines to express its beautiful form.

39

Let the blind see the dance of poetry;
Let the deaf hear the music of poetry.
Let it become the spiritual crutch of the lame, revealing the visible sounds.

40

The breath of wine is fragrant and aromatic,
Regardless of whether it is in a bowl or in a cup.

41
When we are clear that shape is different from form
Poems breathe easily.

42
The four hooves of a galloping horse are released;
The reins of the will are pulled tight.

43
Sometimes the levees are built in vain,
If the roiling water is a flash flood from the mountains.

44
When the wildflowers with their myriad poses are in full bloom across the plains,
I see shapes between each shape.

45
Peacock plumes are gorgeous and multi-colored;
We can only see their beauty in its entirety when the peacock spreads its tail.

46
Logic is contained in images,
But logic is imageless.

47
Mundane thoughts are fragmented;
Theoretical thoughts are complete;
Image-thoughts are concrete.

48
　In the logical thoughts of rational criticism, the essence of objects becomes abstract signs, tying each concept to the others;
　In the image thoughts of the emotional realm, that which has been abandoned is rediscovered, and the different, individual characteristics of each kind of object are restored.

49
　We have been flying in the realm of thought for too long, flying on the borrowed wings of image and concept.
　I picked up their molted feathers; I sought new wings.

50
Poetry comes from outside oneself and from one's heart within—
It is "living," but not always of life;
It resides in images, but it moves into the imageless mists of imagination;
It hides in the shell of "types," but it is untypical and does not belong to Realism.

51
The kind of poetry that expresses "completeness" on many levels is narrative.
Today, the essence of narrative poetry lies in not narrating.
It has destroyed its old nest, spitting upon the despots of incidents, plot, and structure.
Here there are only emotions, emotions that completely open many eyes in an instant.

52
It is a momentary fleeting thought, an unexpected impression.
It is an ever-spinning stormy mass; a riotous, unquietable movement.
It is a meeting on earth, a message broadcast forth from the falling space dust.

53
Poetry is "I"; it is never without my view, heartbeat, or the life-breath of my breathing.

54
Poetry without "me" is false and hypocritical;
In every poem, "I" stand independently.

55
All time and space, movement and harmony, sound and color are here.
I am upon that background.

56

When I express the "existence" in my heart, how can I fear the "non-existence" outside of me?

57

People change; life changes; hearts change; emotions change; poetry also changes.

58

The poetry reading is a characteristic of poetry; perhaps it is one of the primary characteristics in today's modern life. It is not a pose that is struck with an attitude; rather, it is a kind of required action.

If you want to understand the poetry that is being read, you must participate in the audience; you must go to the gathering of the audience, to a large meeting place.

There, under the attentive gaze of the thousands in the audience, the poetry reading spontaneously breathes out its own creative tension and zeal into the atmosphere of the gathering; simultaneously, the poetry reading is also infected by the spicy heat of this living atmosphere.

There, the poetry reading does not belong to any individual but is given to the entire audience. The poetry and the audience are joined as one, melting into one entity.

There, the poetry reading transforms and mutates. In the sensory field of the audience, it becomes a gigantic force. There, and only there, in the heart of the audience does it produce, form, and complete the sculpture of the images of the poem.

60
This is not something that we can sense outside of a poetry reading—
Why are we all wrapped up in a voice full of emotions?
Why do we hold our breaths, panting in rhythm to the poem?
Why, when the poem suddenly demands from us motion, do we all make the same movements as one person, as if we have forgotten ourselves?

61
Only during the poetry reading can you see spontaneity in the roughness, tension in the relaxation, and thickness in thinness.

62
Poetry has architectural beauty of form
And architectural beauty of feeling.

63
    The language here is naked and unadorned.
    This is the only language that can pass through a voice almost as if it is something visible, expressing the individual's hopes and desires that the audience all wants to see. It is oral language which participates directly in life; it is a living script which speaks directly to the audience.

64

    I loudly praise the poetry reading. I think that it is a way of using the voice to explain a thought, a belief, and it is an art which affects society.

    Even more it is magnificent, abstract, and encapsulating;

    It encompasses more space than ordinary poems;

    It uses a thundering voice to form a giant image; it is full of the rich variations of vocal expression; its complete artistic image forms within your sense of hearing.

65

It gathers in the throat all the sounds not yet uttered;
Collecting all the sounds it can make.

66

    Poetry is an active art. In it you must hear the loud footsteps of the era in which the poet lived. Do not just let poetry live in books, upon paper; it must also live in a loudspeaker or in a microphone, so that the chamber music of the poem can dance within the ears of the multitude, striking the gigantic keyboard of the age.

67

Here poetry emerges from the shell of the written word,
And begins to wriggle in the placenta of the voice.

68
Some poems can only be read, and some poems can only be heard.
We want poems that encompass both.

69
The silence of the birds and clouds in the sky is fleeting.
After a moment, I hear the patter of raindrops on the roof.

70
    When poetry presents itself to a mediocre audience, it is like a prisoner being exposed to public ridicule in the stocks.

71
Flattery and debasing both come from ignorance.

72
I heard the drip drop sound of rain,
As it greeted every tender leaf.

73
The one who observes the constellations in the realm of spirit
Will discover new stars.

74
What should I say? What should I think? What should I do?
The important thing is to find where my thoughts are at this moment.

75

We should forever grasp "this moment" at every instant,
A broad new space is rolled up inside of it.

76

Do not hesitate. Just walk inside. This is a marvelous, beautiful realm.

Go visit the Milky Way; go visit the solar system. Go be a tourist on the most distant star.

Grasp a speck of dust, and go discover the bodies of yet-to-be-unfurled new worlds that are tied up within it.

Bring back a piece of meteorite then translate for us the marvelous verses of the universe that are inscribed upon it.

77

If we already know that the Earth is just a beautiful mole,
Should we not go out to clearly see the entire face of the universe?

78

Poetry is most sensitive; I have received its notification—
Millions of suns have exposed the tops of their heads throughout the passing ages.

79

I heard a voice from over there. Every path within the depths of the universe is calling me.

80

    Go forth, my poem.

    Go forth and seek the beautiful memories of our planet that have been stored up for millions of years.

    Go forth and find the earliest shadow left by the wings of human imagination.

81

If there is such a day—
A broad expanse of dark red sky,
The earth like a hot coal, burning white,
Glaciers slowly flowing from the poles to the equator,
And I, the only person left on earth, stretching out a pleading hand to space,
At such a time, poetry will be dead.

The Thinking Soul

(Fragments)

You advocate a scattering of philosophy, returning it to its original state in many art forms. Let us set aside the discussion of philosophy, and examine this from the artistic angle; will you extinguish the uniqueness of art with this act?

--In ancient times, a great philosopher was also a poet and natural scientist. The several branches of scholarship pursued by those philosophers were not clearly separated. Later, the branches of scholarship began to be differentiated. After humans had passed through a long process of knowledge, they felt that there was a danger in philosophy. These solitary forms are less and less helpful in explaining the entire existence of the world and humanity. And now, more and more branches of scholarship are following the trend of unification. The realm of natural science has produced the idea of philosophy; in the realm of the arts, a few great artists are also philosophers. The reason I advocate the return of philosophy to its original state by scattering it among many art forms is because philosophy is plagued with "anemia of ideas"; so far traditional philosophy is all conceptual philosophy. It is mainly directed at the world outside of humans. But today's philosophy is "the philosophy of humans," "the philosophy of images," or the "philosophy of emotions." Art is the most effective form for expressing these kinds of philosophies. After philosophy has been scattered and returned to its original state in art, its independence will be eliminated, and it will be melded into art. Thus, philosophy will participate in and saturate art. It will not affect the independence of the art; on the contrary, philosophy will enrich the art, making it more complex.

April 2, 1983

You say that we should "restore poetry to its original appearance," how do you explain this phrase?

--The first time I accepted all the nakedness of philosophy into a poem, it uplifted the poem, and expanded its capacity. In a certain sense, this is to return to antiquity. Did not the poems of ancient Greece include everything? Does not Western structuralism mention the concept that literature gives a picture of everything?

In one sense, the poems of the past were severed into isolation, especially the poetry of this era that has no philosophy, no music ... Since poetry became a separate kind of literature, it has become isolated, severed poetry.

Restoring poetry to its original appearance refers to poetry reflecting the entire face of the universe.

March 8, 1981

What are your views on the modernization of poetry?

--The modernization of poetry expresses the emotions of the people of this age, and it is seeking or discovering the appropriate form for the expression of these emotions. I must make haste to explain that I am not speaking of emotions in the narrow sense of the word; I have endowed the word with broad connotations so that it includes all the myriad, instantaneous variations of form that occur as the spirit moves.

All poetry is the "corpus of inner activity," expanding out to the universe and then returning to the self. The whole spirit of this activity exists within the "emotions."

November 10, 1981

How do you see the "self"?

----The poet is in independent society. My understanding of the "self" is that it is the "corpus of inner activity." I oppose dividing the self into the man-made distinctions of the "social self" and the "private self." The "self" of a poet is an emotional whole, an enlarged world. Moreover, some people use the angle of sociology to equate the "self" in poetry with individualism for the purpose of killing its character.

How do you see your relationship with the other people of your generation?
----I live among the people of my generation, and I also live apart from the people of my generation. I personally believe that my life extends far in time and space.
What do you think your relationship is to poets of the last generation, such as Ai Qing?

----Blood relatives.

If we look at it from the angle of poetry, their poems are the past of my poems; my poems are the present up to the future of their poems.

How are you different from them?

----Era. Character. Emotions of the heart.

How do you understand poetry and social movements?

----To a poet, any social movement is a poem.

What about poetry and politics?

----Poetry should have politics and philosophy blended into it, but politics should not force poetry onto its tracks.

The universal good of poetry is summed up in one word: independence.

Among the banging sounds of doors closing at the mainland Chinese newspapers and magazines, many from this rising generation of poets have already knocked and entered. It seems that you are the only one left outside the door? Is this so?

----I have also sensed that a warm and welcoming light shines out at me from the cracks of some doorways.

But the door never opens to me.

My name stands alone outside the door.

I feel as if that door is too small, that even if it opened all the way, I would only be able to go inside by turning sideways.

My spirit is an opposing, stable solid.

It is not a balloon that breaks with a "pop."

Nor is it a spring that can be compressed.

It requires a broad emotional space in which to turn freely, from which it can spread out the different facets of poetry's corpus of inner activity.

What is your favorite "poetry"?

----"Heavenly books without words"

It is a book that I have never seen before----

A great secret left by ancient humans;

The mysterious traces from before the appearance of humans and Nature;

It is like the absurdity of the universe that is like Zen but not Zen; and like God's creature that I understand less, the more I read it----"Humanity."

Those books that have already been printed and that will be printed in words cannot and will not have any great magnetic power over me.

Do you like any "poets"?

----All creative geniuses are poets in my heart.

One kind is the famous "great people."

Another kind is the unheard of "great people."

To my view it does not matter if someone is unheard of or famous, they are all "supermen" among the crowd of humanity, as Nietszche said; they are not those who only repeat knowledge without being able to transcend knowledge.

There are very few such people in the entire course of human culture, and they are becoming scarcer and scarcer.

I like aphorisms.

But it does not matter what kind of aphorism it is, as soon as one enters my heart, I begin to repudiate it.

So you mean to say that you only like yourself?

----I am always a stranger to myself.

I must always come to know myself anew in every moment.

And I always discover that I quickly lose interest in myself.

You seem to have a breath of nothingness, is there anything real in human life?

----Nothingness penetrates every person, but not every person has discovered its presence within himself. I bang my head on the gates of existence, and every time I push it open, there is nothingness behind it. Nothingness, oh nothingness! Nothing is real; the only reality is nothingness.

Why do you write poetry or "play" at poetry?

----I said long ago that I only write poetry as a form of "escape." Or perhaps you could say that it is a way of "filling up" the "emptiness."

When you say "emptiness," do you mean what is mentioned in existentialism? When you say "filling up," do you mean the "choice" that they speak of?

----The consciousness of modern humans is woven together with warp and weft. The sensibilities of East and West have a peripheral interchange. Humans have the same "feeling of emptiness" with respect to human life. The difference is that existentialism emphasizes consciously making "free choices" about human life, while I face the "void" of human life with an unconscious "filling up."

Are you a person with a pure spirit? Have you no thoughts of worldly dust?

----"My body creeps upon the dust of the world, but my spirit is in another place." I pursue spiritual purification, and when I am under the control of my abilities and desires, I do my best to escape them by not eating or desiring until I rise to the level of limitlessness.

What do you think "humans" are from the point of view of society?

----"A civilized wild beast."

How do you see humans from the point of view of philosophy?

----A burst of emotion; a burst of disturbance. But regardless if they are emotions or disturbance, all are just what I have previously called "exposed 'nothingness.'"
It cannot be clearly stated if humans should wear signs that say "human" or "inhuman."
Yes, "humans will forever guess about 'humans.'"

What does "weak" refer to when you speak of philosophy?

----It refers to a philosophical relationship between me and the world.

Against the background of "nothingness," how do you regard "name"?

----I must begin with "nothingness."
From the gloominess of human life, I realized the depths of death, and from death I realized the depths of nothingness. It is as if there is a kind of invisible, intangible process there.

In poetry, I was finally "enlightened to see" an intrinsic quality or true meaning that is not related to pure sociology.

The "name" which I grasp so tightly is not simply my own name; its other name is "poetry."

I feel that I am gradually losing support. "Poetry" or "name" is the spiritual support of my life. If I were to lose it, I would feel as if I were "floating aimlessly" or "homeless."

At every moment, every second, I feel as though I am in danger of losing support.

I am just as the spinning "top" that I described earlier, terrified and restless.

In my world----I am just a wailing "frightened mind."

If you never achieve fame during your lifetime and are not recognized until after your death or if even after your death society and the age do not recognize you, what will you do?

----After I am dead, the question "what will I do?" no longer exists because "being recognized" or "not being recognized" do not call to me directly. I do not know if after I am dead, I will be able to discover: "Did I achieve renown?" I have no way to fathom all the mysteries of death.

But while I am living, I must make worthwhile choices with respect to my existence and support those choices with my actions.

I cannot repeat the mistake of my ancestors, who did not attain renown, and put my works of art behind me; I must always place my works of art before me.

If time really must "annihilate" me, my name will struggle to dig through the layers of dirt on my head so that it can see the sky above me.

In the places where my "name" is trampled, I will cause my "name" to continue standing. I will protect my "name", my thoughts, my spirit, until the day I collapse.

But when I strive to transcend the tangible, I only see my "name" in the universe.

Do you hope that people will memorialize you after you die?

----At the very least, I hope that I will not be "forgotten" while I am alive.

How do you view history?

----History is composed of visible and invisible people.
Humans only see the part that is visible.

History is dark; it is a lamp not turned on, one that we turn on only when we need its light. At such times, buried in the darkness of history, we discover large chunks of society, which fell into collapse. In the light, we finally see groups of human beasts, standing, lying, and sitting there. We see the entire spiritual history and development of "humanlike beasts" or "beast-like humans"----the dreamy pastoral songs and the cruel bestial forms, which cannot be harmoniously woven together.

    History only connects with our "needs." At such times, it is no longer a kind of distant abstraction; rather, it becomes a kind of close "emotion," the "reality" or "present" state of our spirit.

    We can say that only our "needs" awaken history, sparing it from being swallowed by the implacable "darkness of forgetting."

    Then, what is art?

    ----Art is subjective emotion. Every kind of art is saturated with the contents of different hearts and emotions. Regardless of the kind of art form we use to express our emotional world, those expressions are merely the outer shell of the emotions and not the emotions themselves; hence, they are not the art itself. They are only the physical label that solidifies or preserves the "memories of emotion" or a kind of "cry" that entices others to enter into the world of the subjective emotion.

May 7, 1983

    How do you essentially differentiate between art as "human emotion" and Croce's "art as intuition"?

    ----Human emotion refers to the "entirety of emotions" in humanity, and it includes intuition.

The intuitions we have about any image are prompted by latent emotions, whether we are conscious of it or not. Because no artist can be completely indifferent and without any "emotion" as he or she receives an intuition about a certain image, the artist in question is "emotionally attached" and not "disconnected."

The images perceived of intuition are generally clear and definite; while the images imbued with emotion are blurred and ever-changing. Modern artists do not simply highlight, explain, and define things; we can say that in their highlighting, explaining, and defining, they are never clear and definite.

The world is what artists strive to grasp but never get a handle on.

If we speak only of intuition, it seems that humans have the richest intuitions during childhood rather than during adulthood or old age. Can we deduce from this that adults and elderly people cannot compare with children in their expression of intuition and in their artistic expression? No. Artists usually have hearts of children, but this refers to their spiritual hearts and does not mean that they have a shallow view of the world. With respect to emotion, the emotions of human artists concerning human life are tied to their spiritual and psychological development. As a person gains deeper experience of the world, his or her spiritual and psychological emotions gain a deeper content day by day, and that person is more able to "attain enlightenment" with respect to certain essentials of human life.

One thing is certain: Any image is imbued with the emotions of the artist, and perhaps the emotions of the artist are impregnated with unknowable images. This is the principal reason that art is art and not pure philosophy.

Croce only affirms art as intuition or art as "spiritual (heartfelt) reality," but he does not include the ability for expression. All people have intuition or spiritual reality, but the difference between them and artists is that artists have a talent for expressing these intuitions or spiritual realities.

Art as emotion is different: The internal essence of art is the psychological or spiritual contents; the outer shell of art is the completed product with form.

May 7, 1983

Bergson also maintains that art is intuition, but you call your poetry (your art) "active art"; in Bergson's view, "the human mind tends towards activities," but most artists have "transcended the control of activity." This is the only way for artists to "escape the curtain of illusion separating humans from reality." They do this by escaping the "knowledge produced by activities" and are not veiled by common knowledge. They do not consider knowledge to be "practical." Instead, they relate directly with reality; therefore, according to Bergson's view are you only an "actor" and not an "artist"?

----That is Bergson, and I am Huang Xiang.
I am a creature of emotions.

I assert that poetry (art) is emotion and not merely intuition. The world is never peaceful, and the endless supply of emotions can find a way here. Emotions mysteriously bind me and externalize themselves as my actions. They require my body to move and do not merely remain in my inner mind. I am always unconsciously directed by these emotions to take this "action" or do that "action." It seems that I am grasping something, but in reality, I am releasing something. This is a kind of psychological anxiety, hysteria, and terror that demands to be "released." It is "not a goal," nor does it point towards a goal. It is "impractical," and it does not serve practicality. It is "irrational," but it is not a kind of blind impulse that appears to transcend rationality. When humans are suffocating, they always find some "air holes" that allow them to breathe.

I want to transcend emotions and the "series of actions" produced by emotions, but as soon as I stop acting, I cannot bear it. Therefore, to me, this "action," which seems to move towards the "goal" of "reason," is not Bergson's "veil of illusion" between humans and reality that has not yet been removed. Neither is it general "knowledge" that serves practicality; rather, it is the universal, biologically significant, true-life "series of emotions" or "emotional radiation" of a social animal.

My poetry is not just a purely spiritual thing; it is also something rooted in my physiology, in the cycle of my emotions. I am never without the sense of the turbulent stillness of the "universal harmony." Every kind of thing that we can see is an integral part of this "universal harmony," saturated with emotions, and a medium for "passing on" emotions. I, too, am an invisible, integral part, vibrating within the universal harmony.

May 7, 1983

Do you agree with Freud's theory of psychoanalysis or Jung's "spiritual vision" and "the collective unconscious"? Which one, or both, can be used to explain you?

----I agree with both of them, but more with the second.

Freud's psychoanalytic theory can be used on many kinds of people; Jung's "spiritual vision" and "collective unconscious" is only applicable to a few people.

I am an ordinary person, and like every person, I am unable to instinctively escape from the physiological characteristics with which I was born. And like some artists, I unconsciously turn my physiological urges into artistic pursuit and impulses. But my physiological consciousness does not disappear; my artistic impulses and pursuits only provide a larger scope for my sexual consciousness.

But I always feel as though I have something that most people do not have. It is a "sense of self-acceptance." I have never been able to become trapped in the ease and rest of "self satisfaction" like most people. Life for me is a never-ending desire. I believe that all my latent desires are also latent in every person. Others do not carefully rid themselves of these desires; they are oblivious to them. They live in a state of numbness and cannot feel the desires. I feel that I am a trembling collection of "silent emotions." When the emotions gain a voice through me, I do not just hear myself, but also my voice combines with the voices of many others. It is not a pure, simple, individual, subjective voice; rather it is a kind of explosive, "collective" voice.

I seek "unlimitedness" and "vastness," even though they are particular "goals" or "meanings" for me.

May 7, 1983

Freud thought that "everyone is a poet at heart; as long as one person lives on earth, poets will not become extinct from the earth." If this is so, what characteristics separate poets and common people? In other words, what is the difference between common people and poets?

----If a person is not a "poet" at heart, he or she is completely a wild beast.

The difference between people and wild beasts is that people pursue their dreams.

I guess that even wild beasts have dreams that people cannot understand.

Every person is most definitely a poet at heart; however, the poets in the hearts of most people are "mutes." The difference between poets and common people is that the poet is "a person who gives voice to emotions."

Do you have Freudian "daydreams"?

----"Fools" and "idiots" all dream by day, but I have the "daydreams" of an "idiot" and a "fool."

I dream by day and by night; there is no dividing line between night and day for me. My dreaming spreads into my entire life. I can say that from my birth to my death, my entire life has been one continuous dream, a dream from which I do not awaken. Only death will be able to awaken me from this great dream. The disturbing, manifest sign of my great dream is found in one word: weakness.

May 7, 1983

Who do you like in the world of music?

----Beethoven. In the past and the present, there is only Beethoven.

When I tire of being entangled by modern artists and abstract thinking, I want to return to Beethoven's majestic, dignified, and solemn world.

Beethoven's art retired to the depths of time, like a quiet, snowy mountain peak.

I still hear a strong, silent call: to unite in love and the brotherhood of humanity, and to once again encourage the belief in human freedom and the invincibility of a good future.

Beethoven's art collected the breaths and views of the millions of people in his era. It expressed the irrepressible pursuit of a people being freed from authoritarianism. Beethoven's view and breath still express our view and breath.

Time cannot quench it.

When I think of Beethoven, I think of his "Ninth Symphony" as a portrait of world history. He describes the people of his era and their lives, their anger and dissatisfaction, their actions, and their business...

Beethoven's music created "Beethoven's hero," who is a representative of free-thinking and an unbending warrior giving no quarter. Beethoven's musical art also expresses the heroic life and the epic of battle. Beethoven's music contains the purity and symmetry of classical sculpture. It has the forceful expression of the marvelous, unlimited variations of rhythm, harmony, and both wind and string musicianship.

Beethoven's art is filled with the great strength of action. His music is a poem of "active art." But I primarily like Beethoven's "person," a roaring, bushy-maned lion in the world of music.

The roars of this earth-shaking lion still sound forth from the disappearances and reappearances of time and space.

Right, how do you see Sartre?

----Sartre, the Frenchman who plays with "existence," is a "brilliant philosophical animal." He causes the people in darkness to discover him. This is why people have given him so many different titles: philosopher, thinker, writer, "great thinker," "bright intellect" ...

Sartre truly has many deep things; he grasps and reveals some of the most essential matters of his era. But other people also grasp the things that Sartre grasps. I once said that the "tips of the psychological feelings" of the East and the West are "woven together three-dimensionally." The difference is that people heard Sartre's "noise," but they did not hear "the East's mysterious silence." In this century, people in both the East and the West are all consciously or unconsciously "freely choosing their lives," and they are externalizing these choices as "actions." Every person in the world knows that he or she should decide what "I should do" or "what I should not do." As a Chinese from the East, I think that while we respect the Frenchman Sartre, we have no need to elevate him into a "Sartre god" to be worshipped. While we respect the great intellect of the French people, we absolutely cannot forget the great intellect of the Chinese people. I am a descendant of the Yellow Emperor; I know that the highest reaches of our philosophy lie in metaphysics; there everything is dark black (or the color of abstraction), of fathomless depths. And the heights of this kind of philosophy are found in the East, not in the West. The East has its Buddhism, its Shakyamuni, and also its Laozi, Zhuangzi, and Zen School. The people of the East have their own holistic way of grasping the world, having created for themselves a kind of quiet, "limitless, primordial" world of acting without doing. It is the rarified essence of human spirit!

In Sartre we see a "disillusioned," "vomiting" person. Sartre is the symbol of "disillusionment" and "vomiting." But, that is only the "mind of Sartre's era," and it is far from being an essential element of the world. When we gain insight into the relationship between humans and the world, we discover that we are "weak."

April 4, 1983

What about Picasso?

----Picasso is a cheater. No, he is a total cheat.

If we say it more politely, he is an illusionist.

Picasso guesses at and plays with the curiosity of the entire world. He gained insight into people's weaknesses, but no one sees through him; on the contrary, people are bewitched by him. In the long-term, he will be torn to pieces by people's "disputes," just like the images in his works.

Speaking from the angle of the history of human knowledge, it can be argued under certain terms that the entire history of art is "bewitching" and "being bewitched," "cheaters" and "the cheated."

We would rather get bewitched, but we do not want to mystify.

Art "bewitches" or "cheats" people, and those who create art also bewitch and cheat themselves.

We want the truth, regardless of the level or significance of that "truth."

We must be given some kind of support; we do not want to become the support for art.

Modern art can be summed up in one word: strange.

Art has developed to the present day, and the "strange" has become prominent. Only the "strange" can attract people, and then you can receive applause from others or get something out of your empty wallet. This is why Picasso became a billionaire.

Picasso created a kind of "Picasso-like person," a type of "infinitive" person, an impersonal person. When we stand in front of the "guessed at" person in a Picasso painting, we spontaneously think of a sentence used in modern philosophy to probe humans: "There is no such person."

Picasso's accomplishment does not lie in setting forth new rhythms of color and line; rather it lies in using "deformation" to ingeniously reveal to people a "possibility" for "humans" and their "circumstances."

Picasso is a person who has not yet been seen to have become the face of the world; he is a rare creature, cloud, bird, beast of art. He is a great artist who uses all sorts of styles and expressive techniques in his paintings.

Picasso, who created a half human, half beast kind of "strange creature," is himself a "strange creature." When we cease our evasion and look on him with astonishment, we will discover that Picasso gives us an "empty" hypothesis.

Second record of conversations with Zhang Jiayan,
editor-in-chief of "The Rising Generation"
April 4, 1983

CONVERSATION WITH AN INVISIBLE "SANCHO PANZA"
—Excerpts from "I Prove Myself"

What was your main reason for planning to write this work?
---"I wanted to prove myself."

I am very interested in your plan. But I do not think there is any reason to put my name on it.
----Our relationship was ordained by history; I am "Don Quixote," and you are "Sancho Panza." We play different roles.

Oh, are we writing and acting in a late twentieth-century comedy?
----Yes. After all the other characters had been taken by others, we could only pick up these two characters to play and to create for ourselves a stage.

Can I ask you, where do you place your "Sancho"?
----He is just my shadow.

Shadow? Does that mean an illusion?
----I am also an illusory being.

If one day, your "Sancho" leaves you, what will you do?
----I have always been alone.

What "windmills" do you face?
----Existence.

What are the implications of the "existence" of which you speak?

----Existence is Noah's ark for the people who are too lazy to live. I do not know whether I will be saved in this ark.

Do you think that since your work appears as a kind of self-proof, it will have a kind of revelatory value?

----The stories in the Bible are based on fabrications, but my strength is based on the truth.

Have you ever been bored?

----I frequently catch flies alone in my room.

What do you think about the entire living human race?

----Foolish like idiots.

And yourself?

----(I had no choice but to reach towards my "shadow" and lazily draw a large "0" with my hand.)

You once said that there is no substantive difference between the death of a king and the death of a rat. What about if you die?

----Oh, in my life, I am also a rat.

Does this mean that you are always hiding here and there?

----Humans have no place to hide on this earth. I am hiding, and I am also fleeing.

Do you think there is a way for you to flee?
----My way is probably the way with no escape.
(We both look at each other without speaking.)

> *Third record of conversations with Zhang Jiayan,*
> *editor-in-chief of "The Rising Generation"*

—From "I Prove Myself"

Is now the time that I have struggled free of "weakness"? Another facet has appeared. Another stage has begun.

Are the things I hazily felt in "Notes Left on Celestial Bodies" the "fables of a new land"?

I once prophesied that one could use color and sound to write poetry and that it is not merely a matter of expressing color and sound within poems. It seems ridiculous. Poetry. Colorful music! Rhythmic painting! The written word limits expression (unfortunately I am as yet only able to use the written word for composing poems); it has much less freedom than color and sound. How does one use the written word to express the things that can be expressed by color and sound? Sound can express feelings; color does not require explanations. The "object" of the non-object is between sound and color. And to use the written word to express a house, you must use the word "house"; to express a night-scene, seascape, or forest, you cannot avoid using the words "night," "sea," and "forest." There is no substitute for them. If you substitute the written word, poetry does not exist. But for music and painting, all you need is sound and color.

The road ... oh, the road ...
Suddenly, at the crossroads of feeling, I meet the "non-object" of abstract paintings and the chaotic "hieroglyphs" of color. There are more difficulties with poetry than with painting. Many, many more difficulties. When the poetry is right, the abstract and the concrete are combined in the poem; Eastern culture and Western culture flow together in the poem ... Painting is not so bad. A few patches of color combined together or blended together thoroughly are "landscape," a very abstract and wonderful product. How can the written word express the abstractness of this kind of landscape? Can it say yellow, blue, black, red? ...

Up to now, my writings have only contained a fable (such as the portrait of "weakness"), a symbolic fable. How do I express an abstract fable? A "fable" of a non-fable?
The more I move forward, the more I need to get rid of the written word; at the very least I must shatter the original "form of meaning" of the words, causing them to express their highest essence, which had been previously ignored in the world of appearances.

November 15, 1982

To express the innermost human heart, one cannot rely on "the form," but only on "the divine." "The divine" is always moving; it is hard to grasp and ever-changing.
Everyone can see the different "gods" flowing within or floating behind every matter.

In a pile of lonely days, my writings explore the marvelous scene outside the world; in the condensation of cross-eyed vision I laid hold of the inward potential appearance of the world, and I rolled them together into a new "freedom." Suddenly, it was as if a ray of strong light swiftly passed before my eyes, and immediately disappeared. But this was only for an instant. I discovered a world pressing close to me that had never existed before and that I had never seen in my poems.
November 15, 1982

Free color like a painter,
Free sounds like a musician,
Poet, you should "free the written word."
Right!
　"Free the written word,"
The written world should seek freedom from the "formal meaning" that it originally had.
November 16, 1982

If modern poets want to free poetry, they must start by freeing the written word!
November 16, 1982

"Freeing the written word" should be the "loudly imaginative" banner of modern poetry.
November 16, 1982 at night

Allowing the written word to construct an image is a reverting to hieroglyphs in its release.
November 16, 1982 at night

Thoroughly dig out the potential that can be expressed by the written word.
Allow the object of poetic expression to become abstract (this abstraction is not the same as the speculative abstraction in pure philosophy, but possesses the flow chart of a changed image).
I discovered that the latent language of color and lines (the rotating sounds of brightness and color, the rhythm in lines) can be used in poetry.
It makes the entire poem become an unpredictable "rotating hieroglyph."
December 2, 1982

In sum, poetry still has no choice but to receive help from the written word; however, it must transcend and free the written word.

A new artist is a new "content," a kind of new "future language." His psychological and spiritual message is outside our accustomed cultural form.

December 2, 1982

It is the same as simplifying our characters; the language of poetry itself should boldly simplify and formalize. Spirit is formality, and formality is formless.

December 16, 1982

The source of all spiritual suffering among humans is the sedimentary deposit of culture. No animals have this. Animals only have physical suffering but not spiritual suffering. Poetry also has a kind of suffering—the accumulation of language.

Primitive humans, living in mist and amazement, are more able to come close to the heavenly bodies and the great earth. That is a rounded world without edges.

Artists should bring back the same, but not necessarily the same, purity of the primitive spirit.

January 1, 1983

Majestic poetry has its own dignity.

It despises humanity's shallowly fashionable language of the earth's stones.

It is quiet.

Creators of great poetry are like great sculptors; they do not get side-tracked into making carvings of insects.

December 1, 1982

Poetry contains and transcends the "intelligence" of time and space.

It is not measured or limited by the "intellect" framed in time and space.

It is not a measure, but diffusion.

September 20, 1985 at night

I no longer want to fathom the image of poetry, but rather the abstract image of poetry, or the "abstract image." I create a kind of poetic "hieroglyph" containing an immense spirit.

September 20, 1985 at night

The philosophical language of poetry is a blurry, unclear philosophical language. The philosophy of poetry is a blurry philosophy, an emotional philosophy.

Poetry presents a face of philosophy that is a blurry, emotional face. The more you look into the depths of this face, sober awareness gradually disappears. This face is fully covered with a misty, hidden, latent awareness.

This is a very deep face.

It leads you level by level into the approach to the dusky depths of the world's essence.

September 20, 1985

The Eastern mysticism of poetry is a kind of divine rhyme, an atmosphere, and not an explanation. It resembles Eastern philosophy in the significance of "enlightenment." But the "enlightenment" of poetics is not just profound thinking; even more, it is a direct grasp of the emotions included in the world of images. Poetry integrates, disappears, and sublimates in all kinds of Eastern philosophies. Poetry is not like Buddhism in its lack of concern for the origin of the world and the divine nature while only focusing on the situation of "suffering" humans and on the source of sufferings and the way to escape them. Neither is poetry Daoism, with its aspiration to discover the limits of the world of the Dao and its difficulties in determining "reality," unveiling the natural order and the process and the way in which the universe moves and then demanding that human actions spontaneously accommodate the way of the universe and escape the strict rules of humanity in their accommodation of Nature. Poetry is not a religious prayer, nor is it a magic ritual.

In certain significance, poetry is even far from myth, despite the fact that it can never leave the mythic form of expression. Preaching is a taboo to poetry even though poetry often versifies rational arguments.

Poetry is such a thing; you enter the world from a certain place, suddenly opening this empty room of the world. Inside it is pitch black and icy cold; you spontaneously cry out: "Who, centipede?" Poetry is this sudden "shout," a sudden "light" in the inky blackness.

September 20, 1985 at night

The poetic art is the same as other arts; its eternal, unchanging law is "discovery" and not "repetition." It is not a "filling up" of past cultures; rather, it is a "climbing along" into new cultures.

Poets must have their own spiritual histories.

They should not just borrow outward spiritual shells from others to "fill" up their own content.

September 20, 1985

The creation or completion of the spiritual world of poetry must and can only be based on "independence" of character: true, disorderly, harmonious independence.

September 20, 1985 at night

The way in which modern poetry changes the order of time and space should not merely be a changing of the rhythm of time and space, but also it should principally be a change in the nature and concept of time and space. If you only change the rhythm of time and space, it is still the original time and space. Its essence has not been moved in the least. Such a change is utterly outward and shallow. Breaking through the nature and concept of time and space is to build on a new philosophical foundation. Those who can form their own poetic philosophy are the truly great poets.

September 20, 1985 at night

The highest image of modern poetry is not an image contrasting with a background, which is also a material, practical, easily grasped image; rather, it is an "abstract image."
Such images do not need to be differentiated as images in contrast to the background. Instead, they are "blended into" the background; they are images discovered latently in the background itself and even images dug out from behind the background.

"The background is the image."
Behind the background there are also latent images.
These things are extra-sensory.
They are in the appearance of the world's hidden, naked body, and they are also hidden behind the appearance.

September 20, 1985 at night

Now ... here ... it is so marvelous:
Hidden, yet naked. Naked, yet hidden.
The world is not only naked before us in a hidden way. It is also hidden from us in a naked way.

April 23, 1985

Poetry without "spiritual discovery" is not creative poetry;
Poets without "spiritual discovery" are not true poets.
Poets who only play with techniques cannot touch the spirit. Pure technique is merely fluff. We demand that poems have the "spiritual capacity" of independent existence. Poetry without large capacity cannot be considered a great masterpiece.
In saying this, we do not oppose the pure beauty of any specific poem.

September 20, 1985

Poetry does not only display an ancient trigram, a bronze myth, or a legend carved on a tomb. Nor does it display the disappearance of the "ruins" and "monuments" of time and space. Instead, it should be a "multi-faceted corpus of inner activity," a "spiritual universe of my own body" in this moment.

September 15, 1985

The modernization of historical poetry depends on:
Its not being annals, but a spiritual picture of the world;
Its not being a concrete narrative, but an abstract lyric;
Its not being a congealed "lump," but a flowing "fragment."
Each individual fragment constitutes an entire "wholeness," and together they are strung into one entity, simultaneously pounding and disintegrating the "totality" of the whole;
It is not a flood of "zealous" words, overflowing into expression, but the coolness of the philosophical discourse behind the zeal, refined and concise;
It is not the flowing "appearance" in songs, praise, exposure, and curses, but the emotional intuition based in poetry that examines and transcends all in profound thought and understanding.
Its master is not a visible "person";
Rather, it is a disappearing, invisible "spirit."

September 15, 1985

The elevation of poetry is always the process of disappearing the concrete expression of a lower level. It keeps the things from the highest preceding level, where it is hard to clearly distinguish between the concrete and the abstract.

September 15, 1985

The highest level of Eastern culture is not "emotional culture"; rather, it is the lonely "spiritual culture." This kind of culture is reviving in contemporary poetry.

March 19, 1986 at night

We should no longer cut apart a poem into content and form. The spirit of the poem does not merely manifest itself in the content, but also it manifests itself in its "spiritual form."

March 19, 1986 at night

O, China! O, Far East!
Do you only want to display to the world your bodies in sports without also proudly displaying to the world your ancient spirit of wisdom?

March 19, 1986 at night

In creating poetry do not simply learn to worship others; if we ardently aspire to worship, why can we not turn our blind worship of ancestors and powers to the worship of our own bodies and spirits?

March 19, 1986 at night

There is no center in the kingdom of poetry.
Do not think that the center is a reliable, fixed point. You are

standing in a directionless flow, and the "center of this circle" is also its circumference.

March 19, 1986 at night

I say to you that if you are a ghost, you do not need to play at being a ghost. If you are not a ghost, do not pretend to be a ghost and scare others. The attractive power of poetry is in its truth. The depths of poetry are in its sincerity.

March 19, 1986 at night

If we look at a poet from the aspect of "humanity," then without a doubt: disposition is more important than talent.

March 19, 1986 at night

What is poetry?
Humans! Gods! Devils! Beasts!

March 19, 1986 at night

If you want a creative spirit, you must first possess a spirit. If you have not had a true inner journey, if you do not have your own spiritual experiences, how can you "possess a spirit"? It is impossible. Do not affect poses, or pretend to mystify people. Just look at those people!
However, I really do like "mystery."

March 19, 1986 at night

At first glance, mystery is "empty,"
On closer examination, mystery is "marvelous."
March 19, 1986 at night

I am here! Drinking alone, there more than a thousand people shouting, "nothingness."
March 19, 1986 at night

Oh, the imagination is so withered and astringent! Oh, the sensibility is so weak! Have you "seen" and "heard" the great "black mirror" of the earth?
It hangs high in your rising human bodies. Do not turn a blind eye to it.
Do not turn a deaf ear to it.
It is a ray of invisible "light" that will not be silenced;
It is a pulse of inaudible "noise" that will not be extinguished.
March 29, 1986 at night

Turn your view back upon yourself; look, in the darkness there, hidden beauty is revealed.
March 29, 1986 at night

It is like a riddle.
A person, such as I, throws into the world just a few roars and makes a few actions.
At the same time, I play with metaphysics, tragedy, transcendence, existence, and emotions.
I discovered that people play with themselves.

This is too boring, and I always scream out loud!
When I turn over and look,
I suddenly discover Zen, I-ching, Laozi ...
One, such as I, writes poetry, does tai-chi,
The writings and limbs of a relaxed animal.

August 4, 1985

In poetics, the way to beg is to plagiarize.

So why does he attack others? Because he is jealous; why is he jealous? Because he is weak.

Self-confidence is so valuable! So many of us lack this thing; however, whenever self-confidence becomes blind, you do not even see yourself clearly.

Oh, who is that? It seems that I have seen him somewhere. See how that "self-confidence" is so excessive; see how he is talking to himself again ...

Poetry has a magical beauty and a Zen beauty, even if the poet is not a magician or a Zen master.

If poetry were just the crazy juxtaposition of words, then there would be twenty billion poets among ten billion people. Even the unborn children should be counted as poets. Even the dead should be counted as poets.

Ravings are not enlightenment; in poetry we do not reject ravings.
Strange howls are not tiger roars; such bursts of excitement are merely a tiger's pelt.

A sudden, strange whistle will scare people speechless and bug-eyed, but the second time they hear it, the people will learn to do it.

If you are going to scream, then scream one time! If you are going to scream, then use your tone!

What is not beautiful about exaggerating, speaking crazy words, or speaking nonsense?
If you really have understood a certain inexpressible thing in your heart, then poetry overflows with magical color or deep Zen meanings.
Such chaos is very similar to furor, but furor belongs to creative genius! Apery is pretending to create something new, but people have already discerned what is real and what is fake.

After being released from the calculations of mathematics and geometry, we recover the "intoxication" of ancient chaos; After being elevated above the level of various complicated feelings, we climb close to the great purity of emotion.

When did "modernism" become a kind of fashionable illness? Look at all those people crawling around in confusion; the illness has become incurable.

That "modern man" sits there silently with his head down and without any expression on his face. He does not find it strange that no one knows him, even though he knows you; he does not feel bad that no one knows him, even though he still holds fervent hopes for humanity.

All right! Let's compromise. I also like "modernism," but I like your father. I like the "first" of any "school"! I despise and hate any followers. They are like the scavenging hyenas behind a giant beast.

Do you not see that your "poetry" is spattered with the semen that dripped off of others?

Creation is always a matter for the few, a matter for individuals among the few;
You do what you what you ought.
What do the affairs of others have to do with you?

Have you truly felt the mystery?
It is difficult to move on from feeling to grasping; it is also difficult to move on from grasping to expressing, but you have not yet even felt it!

The thinking soul is cut off.

There is a sudden silence.
The miserable silence is an eternally miserable fish that conceives me inside it.

The Waterfall of the Human Body

It is a common scenic place.
But its name thunders, rings throughout the world. It is famous in all countries.

It is like an undeservedly famous person, whose name "thunders" among humanity, but when you meet him in person or look at his works, you feel that they are common, and you might even be disappointed. In the end, it is just a "freshet without much water."

The Huangguoshu Waterfall gives me such a feeling.
A river is broken by a cliff, and several streams of water fly straight down over the bare rock face like a white curtain, like the scattered tufts of white hair on the bald head of time. The entire Huangguoshu Waterfall gives me this impression: It feels like the exhaustion and languishing of life. Perhaps it was the dry season for the falls. But even if it had been full of water, what more would there be? Just greater quantities of water and more noise. Even when you stand before Niagara Falls in America, your "human body" will not "be shaken by it," I think.
People are always curious about the world's famously beautiful scenic places, which they have not seen. This is the common psychological situation of the human race. But once they have seen a place, the beauty of the place decreases greatly, or even vanishes completely. Just like when people stand before Huangguoshu Waterfall; for most of the tourists, it is just a matter of "the water does its thing, and I do my thing." There

are very few "human bodies that are shaken by it." The average person, at the most, will show a little interest on a later date after eating and drinking his fill, and will superficially boast: "Oh, I have seen the Huangguoshu Waterfall!"
So what if you have seen it? Seeing it is just seeing it. Before you see it, you are curious, and after you have seen it, you are no longer interested. This person's world lacks a long-term shock.
This is the reason that the people living near the Huangguoshu Waterfall are used to it and indifferent to it. They have lived with the noise of the falls for a long time; they even live at the top of the Huangguoshu Waterfall, and so they no longer see or hear the falls. They face the great waterfall, and yet it is as if they do not see the falls. The noise of the large waterfall inundates them night and day, but it is as if they do not hear it. The waterfall does not surprise them, it does not move them spiritually, nor does it shake the days of their lives.

The waterfall just seems like an ordinary person among them, squeezed in between their bodies. It exists apart from them, and no one thinks of paying attention to it.
Perhaps, the people living near the Huangguoshu Waterfall have become numb to such marvelous scenery; they are too accustomed to it! Day after day, they face the waterfall, and they are tired of hearing it! Tired of seeing it!
Perhaps the waterfall itself is tired.
The waterfall disappeared for humans.

It hopes that people will rediscover it.
It is strange. The first time I saw the Huangguoshu Waterfall, I immediately felt tired.
I stood before the waterfall, and it was as if I had never seen it; in the roar of the waterfall, it was as if I did not hear it.
Is life tired?
Is it because I was hoping to be shaken with a kind of new life? Does such a shaking come from outside of me or from inside of me?
After an instant, I felt: In reality, I am looking at a waterfall without a waterfall and listening to a waterfall without a waterfall. I placed myself into the sound of a soundless waterfall. The waterfall was in front of my feet, over my head, to my right, and to my left. The waterfall was facing me from above, below, right, left, and all directions. I erected the waterfall as a pillar. My entire body felt the moisture. It turned out that the sound of the waterfall came from inside me. My life instantly filled with water.

A flying waterfall of the human body is hanging out over the void of the background.
Nothing can make me excited.
My body is the excitement of the flowing waterfall.
At this time, even if someone were to move in a most startling manner and do a somersault while jumping off the top of Huangguoshu Waterfall as everyone was watching, and then fall into the deep lake below, causing shock, uproar, and commotion, I would definitely not participate in the shock, uproar or commotion.

I already consider the movement and form of the external world to be common occurrences.
"Movement" is not completed by moving;
"Form" is not shaped by forming.
The appearance of the world or the apparent world can no longer excite me.
If at this moment someone jumped from the top of the waterfall into the deep lake below, then, the one jumping from the top of the waterfall is I. I fall into my body.

People only see the waterfall outside themselves. They look at it all day long, and in the end, it makes them indifferent. People do not instead think that there is another waterfall that eternally excites. It might be hidden behind you or in a cave where you cannot see it. It is a "cave" that the average person cannot discover or enter into. There, only the mysterious "rat" can come in and go out. It is a place off the beaten track.
That cave is the water curtain cave of the human body.

The entire human body is a waterfall cascading mysteries to you. This is a place of extremely ordinary yet highly mysterious scenery. It has both the life of shallow water and the change of rising water. But during its season of low water, the volume of flowing water does not decrease; during its season of rising water, the volume of flowing water does not increase.
It is constant water that never increases or decreases.
It is a forgotten place of "human" scenery. It hangs there without tiring outside the view of easily tired humans.

The eternally roaring, dark night of the waterfall of the human body.

Six Topics on Poetics

EXTREMITY

In a certain sense, personality is a kind of "paranoia," a kind of extreme position; creating something new is the denial of one extreme position by another extreme position. For example, Dostoyevsky was a masochistic "paranoiac"; Nietzsche's extremely aggressive philosophical spirit contradicted the "extremes" of Schopenhauer's pessimism.

But every kind of extremity is not an absolutely extreme position. For example, all kinds of extremities reflect to differing extents different kinds of personalities, and every kind of personality is manifested in a complete world of its own that is self-satisfied and self-attained.

Every kind of personality has its source, its flowing river of a body, and its ever-broadening "river mouth where it flows into the sea."

One kind of personality does not reject another kind of personality. In other words, the "river mouth" of one personality does not drown out the "river mouth" of another personality.

Every personality has its own source, river body, and river mouth.

Creativity absolutely requires personality.

It does not matter what kind of personality you have; you include the entire world from the angle of your personality. If we compare this to colors, it is like a certain shade of "yellow." This "yellow" is not the absolute, pure yellow, despite the fact that it can be distinguished from other colors. Rather, this "yellow" includes other colors such as red, blue, green, white, and black. It only manifests the basic characteristic of "yellow" in the light. "Black" is the same. "Black" is not absolute, pure black. It also has all the other colors in the world blended into it, and "black" is merely its basic form of expression.

Our physical eyes cannot usually see all the other colors included in black; only the wise eyes of our spirit can see the "hidden bodies" of all the spots of other colors in "black."

Colors possess the capability of infinite variation.

Any color can be mixed to make millions of other colors, with infinite variations.

Absolutely "pure" things transcend human sight.

Can there be an absolutely pure color in the world? No! Just as the original color of a color, which includes all the other colors mixed into it, cannot represent all the other colors but can only represent itself. The "personality" of color expresses itself. Any one personality cannot cancel out all the other personalities; instead, each personality exists independently in the world.

Without different "extremes" there can be no different personalities.

Without different personalities there can be no different worlds; however, each real personality has the capacity of its own world and the world's capacity.

Originality is the overall content of the world in a certain personality; it is not that the world accommodates this personality and engulfs it.

In this sense, "extremity" is not the absolute, pure extreme. Extremity is "not extreme." Absolute "purity" is to transcend one's own existence, and one's own existence cannot be transcended.

CONTROL

There is an argument that says that great poets are all good at controlling themselves; they are good at moderating or controlling their passions and talents.

But passions and talents are not the waters of a river; they are the flow of life.

They do not require a river bed, nor do they need people to build strong dikes to control them.

Enormous talents and passions are the rushing, overflowing flood of life, flowing out in all directions. They cannot be steered or swum across. They sweep you up and drown you all, including those who stand on the bank trying to calmly observe the flow of human life and those who possess genius and passion.

This is why those who create with their lives must "die" while creating; they must "die" countless times while they are creating, and from "death" they receive new life. Their creations are not the pure, recreational pursuits of "gentlemen," which are made in a state of emotional calm and quiet. Their creations are pieces of their own flesh dropped onto the page and into their words; they are the drops of their blood that seep into their pens and saturate their words.

Each process of creation is a casting down of one's whole life.

The flow of life is the flow of flesh, the flow of blood, the flow of marrow! It is the concentration of essence and blood, the quivering of brain and nerves, the externalization of the heart's rhythmic beating.

Creation is a kind of extreme mania, an excited state of obsession; it is the entire person in a particular moment or in a certain stage, "investing" everything once for all. Such an "investment" holds back nothing, and in reality it can never be repaid.

Those who understand creating "without experiencing it for themselves" cannot explain creating. They think that "a calm, controlled state" is the best creative state (but in reality that is a better state for "self-cultivation"); presenting a "calm, controlled creation" is the most ideal creation (but in reality it is a bland, weak "creation" that is distanced from life).

When full of such "un-imagination," when the unimaginative technician wells up, then they have a few ordinary opinions.

This is the "creativity" of those who do not know how to create.

They cannot understand those who are "martyred for creativity" when creating something. They can never understand why the cursive masters of antiquity would run and shout while doing their calligraphy or why they would dip their heads in the ink and write with their hair in an "uncontrolled" state. Neither can they understand why the ancients, when they wrote a good poem, would be unable to stop themselves from ringing all the temple bells in the middle of the night, scaring all the residents of the capitol with their craziness.

They are the modern, pedantic "baccalaureates" who "chew" on life; they are the "lovers" of pretentious, arty "critics" of calligraphy and paintings.

They do not see the lightning of essence and blood! They do not hear the roaring waves of human flesh!

A madman can never fully learn "control."

A shaker can never be completely "moderate."

Life is rich with moving feelings. Art that expresses life is the same; even quiet, gentle art has an atmosphere of invisible "movement" hidden in it.

A tendency to frozen "moderation" is the road to death. Absolute moderation is death itself.

"ALIENATION"

Do you think that a "modern poet" cannot leave modern "culture"? Do you think that a temperament and character of insanity, paranoia, and animal-like violence is not a modern "cultured poet's" "cultured condition"?
Do you think that throwing one's entire being into creative activity, making life into poetry and making poetry into life are the "alienation of genius from genius" in the modern realm of creativity?
The poet is always a free citizen in the kingdom of his spirit. He is not a model of "culture" and "education."
The poets of any age always transcend the "highest standards and ethical norms" of the age in which they live.
It does not matter how time changes or how the eras change, the lifestyle of a poet revolves around himself. He always firmly adheres to his own life's nature and reality.
The poet is least likely to "adjust" himself to popular customs for the sake of accommodating others; he always transcends the fashions of his era.
This is the natural "poetic" temperament that is reflected in the person of the poet!

Therefore, the poet is always "unpopular"; he always walks alone, independent of the "fashions" and "customs" of his era.

Both in ancient times and modern times, poets are those with the strongest life-forces, the people who "live the longest";

no poet with a strong life-force merely belongs to his own age. Poets are always lonely. They are like "lonely beasts" surrounded by humanity. Their inner hearts are crashing with violence and terrible things. Their violent, terrible, crashing inner hearts cannot be tolerated by others; it is even hard for them to tolerate themselves.

Hence, poets always "suffer." They bear the great sufferings of all humanity; they have the spirit of martyrs. They are forever being "exiled."

Their spirits are always "moving forward." They do not live near the "common customs," nor do they make friends with "ease." They exile themselves into the freedom of exile.

They are always strange in their character and temperament. Psychologically, those with ordinary mental illnesses look upon them as "sick" and in need of the cure of "dominating enlightenment."
Their natural psychological temperament is in accord with nature.
They receive from nature large amounts of freedom.
They naturally "change in an instant," just as thunder and lightning can suddenly appear in a clear sky, or as the calm ocean can suddenly be roiling with waves.
The waves, thunder, and lightning of poets is always "natural." I can never be controlled by humans or "arranged."

This is the free life that melds together the heavens, the earth, and all things.

To those who strictly organize life, creativity, entertainment, work, rest, and even emotions, the poet's state of existence is unfathomable; it is even the "fatal weakness" in the meaning of existence.

Poets are the sovereigns of life, but not the "managers" of life. Life and creation are the same to them; they do not have any manmade boundaries.

Creation is all! Creation is over all! Creation is life itself!

This is the highest state of intoxication—"always drinking without getting drunk"—that most people in ordinary circumstances cannot experience or fabricate.

In this Dionysian state, poets receive unusual ecstasy and blessing. This is the state of their lives, and it is a life-style that appears to be one of "self-alienation" in the eyes of ordinary people.

But poets never feel that there is "any alienation" in their lives. What are they "alienated" from? Why are they "alienated"? What is "alienation"? They only know creation! Creation! Their entire life is an existence of creation.

Poets are the only people not wearing the cloak of culture among the "cultured creatures" of cultured society.

They do not decorate themselves with culture.

To humanity that enjoys the "culture" of modern society, poets still belong to a culture of "ignorance."

FLOW

The creative activity of a great artist or a great poet does not move upwards in a straight line, nor does it move in never-ending cycles.

Their entire creative work is a process. And every stage of the entire process is sufficient to itself; they all have the appropriate height for that particular stage.

It is not wise to divide up the members of the entire body of an artist's or a poet's creative activity through "agglomeration" or through "putting into lines." Creation is not a machine, and it cannot be mechanically put together or taken apart. Every part of it, every stage is connected to the others and is permeated with and permeates the other stages. It is difficult to clearly divide this chaotic mass into "clear lines of flow."

Each part of it simultaneously "participates" in another part.

When we look at the "spiritual flow" of a great poet or great artist, we can never clearly indicate the direction of the flow and the exact positions of its beginning and end.

A spiritual flow is a psychological flow. It is a phenomenon of life without position.

Its gradually widening "mouth to the sea" is also its "mouth from the sea." It is a roaring flow. It is the deafening, lonesome sound of the world.

Its turbulent "flow" is a kind of "turbulent calm" or a "calm turbulence."

Its "flow" in any place has a hidden, invisible "source"; there, every place can have a source for a new flow that never needs to be sought and that you find unexpectedly.

BREATH

"Breath" is the electricity of life. It is the electricity of universal emotions.

When a person dies, he "stops breathing." His "electricity goes out."

Hence, life hinges on "breath." "Breath" moves the circulation of blood and makes our muscles flexible. Breath moves our heart and pulse. It causes the entire flesh-and-blood mechanism of the human body to function.

Without "breath," the blood stops circulating and congeals; the muscles loosen and decay; the heart and pulse stop their rhythmic beating. All of life itself weakens and dies.

"Breath" makes life "move"; it fills the human body with organic function.

The heavens have air—"heavenly breath"; the earth has its "earthly breath"; humans have "human breath."

The changes of light and shadow are the "heavenly breath"; the changes of the seasons are the "earthly breath"; emotional changes are "human breath."

The human body is a "breath furnace," a "breath storehouse." The atmosphere echoes the crossflow of the universe's "breath field." Everything abounding with creative life is the masterpiece of the "breath of the universe," which we sense but cannot see.

All great poets and artists are the immortal sculptures of the "breath of the universe." Their works of art contain echoes of the atmosphere and are filled with the essential breath, original breath, blood and breath, and divine breath of life!

Poetry and works of art "without breath" are counterfeits.
The makers of such counterfeits are false poets and artists.
Because their works do not have life "thrown" or "poured" into them, when life passes through their words, lines, rhythms, melodies, colors, and words, it becomes a form "without any breath." Such works, no matter if they are poems, paintings, sculptures, dances, or music, are all works "without breath."
If they express themselves in philosophy, especially in poetic philosophy, then it is also philosophy "without breath."
If we measure poetry and all works of art according to "breath," then we are measuring poetry and art according to life. Such poetry and works of art possess a life that is waiting for us to dig it out.

"Breath" transcends time and space.
It should be an important symbol of contemporary poetics.
It does not distinguish between traditional and modern; nor does it differentiate between Chinese and foreign. "Breath" can only belong to **humanity, life, and existence.**
"Breath" resides in language, and it also wanders outside the realm of language.
It exists in the "realm without words."

Those pure, "cultured" modern pedants are people without "breath," especially the pedants of poetry.

Ancient China's art of calligraphy had "uncultured," crazy "men of breath." In a state of furor, surrounded by flowing breath, they created works of calligraphy and painting, which were full of breath.

The "breath" of all art comes from the "breath" of life.

Essentially, human culture is a kind of "breath culture." The form of expression does not matter; the changes and variations among schools of style do not matter. All the variations do not depart from "breath."

The spirit in poetry is the long-winded breathing of the epic. "Breath" is the basic, unchanging, important aesthetic symbol and aesthetic characteristic of human art from antiquity to the present. It does not matter how art changes in form; art cannot banish "breath" to a place outside of itself.

A person without "breath" is dead; art without "breath" is cold and dead. "Breath" is rounded, uniting. Things without "breath" are "deflated."

Even the death depicted in art is not death itself; rather, it is life with breath.

"Breath" causes heliospheric transpiration, keeps plants green, and makes all things abound with life.

The lives of great people with spiritual enlightenment, creators, and revolutionaries are themselves a great "breath field"; people with a weak breath of life or slow breathing cannot connect to the breath within them.

But the "breath (*qi*)" of which I speak here cannot be confused with the narrow meaning of "*qigong*". It absolutely is not merely a matter of strengthening one's body and cultivating oneself to the point of attaining the mystical state of "acting without doing" (*wu wei*); rather, it refers to gathering the atmospheric flows of life and breaking ground in the "field" of the life of the universe. In this significance, all great poets, great artists, and great thinkers harvest the heavens, the earth, and all things; they are those who gather the essence of the sun, the moon, the mountains, and the rivers within themselves. They are wondrous people, "breath people," who are impregnated with the universe. They are not *qigong* masters in the world of *qigong*. Their true "special skills" are writing poetry, composing music, drawing pictures, and making thoroughly mysterious spiritual creations.

TWO-FOLD HARM

Our age has entered into a totally absurd stage: on the one hand, it is crowned with the restoration of "traditional" culture; on the other hand, it is called the "pioneer" of proliferating weak, pseudo-cultural phenomena.

We must oppose both these things.
The true significance of Chinese culture lies in the cracks between these two, where it is on the brink of suffocation and cannot spread out.
Real poets have become the two-fold victims of two kinds of "culture."
They are under two kinds of pressure and are oppressed from both sides.
They have almost no way to fit in with several generations of readers. The general spiritual space has become the shallow "cave" culture, the "*yangko*" culture. Popular culture and even a "culture" of cultural counterfeits fill up almost everything…
Such a situation still continues, and it will have the disastrous result of killing the spirit of the people. It has almost become a tragedy from which there is no escape…
And "being caught in the cracks" does not mean that culture is in a "canyon" where it is "beaten by warm waves."
Nor is it in a field of "fertile soil" from which it can "grow" a "cultural landscape" for this age.
It is simply caught in the cracks; it is "caught in a crack," which is growing narrower and narrower. Modern Chinese

culture is being "squeezed to death" between new and old, right and wrong, light and dark. It does not develop, nor can it ever develop, if it is a marvelous spiritual scene that is really "traditional" or truly "pioneering." It can only produce shame and the bitter desolation of the people's spirit.

The Thunder of Deep Thought

—Poetic Philosophy
(1981-1992)

EMOTIONAL PHILOSOPHY
—Modern "Poetics" I

I am only expressing to you a kind of transcendent experience, a kind of image, a kind of attitude that my "whole being" experienced in an instant. If you take it as theory, it will immediately reject you...

----Can what you refer to as "emotional philosophy" be received by people's common sense?
----Emotional philosophy is not the speculation of extraordinary perceptions; however, neither is it something, which common sense cannot receive under normal circumstances. Emotional philosophy is the opposite of traditional "conceptual philosophy," and it raises a new question. Perhaps, I am only raising a new question, but it is not its ultimate perfection.
----Then, what are the "emotions" of which you speak?
----Emotion is the ancient riddle that puzzles the world.
The emotions mentioned here have broad psychological content. They are not the psychological reactions that are opposite to reason and distinct from feelings, which are usually discussed in psychology. Rather, these emotions refer to all irrational, natural psychological surges and processes, which change ten thousand times in an instant and which any human has under normal circumstances.
Emotions are the **turbulence** of the mystery of life, **the natural desires and passions**, which **cannot be fathomed**; they disturb our calmness and tranquility.

----What about "emotional philosophy"?

----This kind of philosophy has the sense of not coming from cultural traditions, not being of human making. It explains the world apart from the view that humans are the main subject. It naturally returns to humans themselves, and from the turbulent surges and processes in life, it explores and discovers the true meaning of philosophy.

----What is the significance of such a philosophy?

----This philosophy returns to the basics.

Its goal is to boldly restore to itself the research category of "humanity" that has been banished from philosophy. Its core is humanity, gestating within the world. Its highest form of expression is "poetry," including poems, poetics, poetic philosophy, poetic aesthetics, and universal religion in verse.

All previous philosophies have form, but emotional philosophy is "formless." All previous philosophies begin with the individual and move out into the world; emotional philosophy begins with the world and returns to humanity itself. Philosophy of the past came from the outside; modern philosophy comes from the inner heart, from the self. Just as it is absurd to explain the world apart from humanity, so also it is absurd to explain humanity apart from the world.

Monologue of "Emotions"

Emotional philosophy denies the truth, certainty, and stability of an "object."

It first denies the truth of things. It denies the truth of language expressing things. It denies the truth of all kinds of concepts that are constructed by human language.

All traditional philosophy is composed of concepts secreted by the brain; it is bound up in the web of sticky concepts.

There is no "truth" in concepts.

The things that we see are a kind of false image.
It is not "it," but rather, another thing.

Emotional philosophy does not receive any rational "basic laws" or "basic principles" that are rooted in logic or reasoning.
The world is not a conceptual image designed by the human brain.
The world is an emotional process, a changing flow of emotions. It does not call to or respond to the human brain, but to the human spirit. It is not a rational image designed by the human brain. Rather, it is an "emotional" picture, which is ever-changing and constantly flowing, that resonates with the spirit.
There is no world of "natural laws." A "principled" world does not exist.
There is no world of all kinds of "gods"; such a world just does not exist.

There are only the time and space of the process; there are only the form and shadow of the process; there is only the material image of the process.
"Emotions" do not exist, nor are they non-existent. They "exist" between being and non-being.
They are always someplace, but I am unable to tell you with certainty exactly where they are.

All forms are the sense of "emotion." They are all the instantaneous expression of "emotion."

"Emotion" is process, tendency, and flow. It lies between "emotional" and "unemotional."

Universal emotions are the outward expression of "nothingness."

The next instant will never again live in the previous instant. In every second there is a certain state; every state is an emotion with which you resonate.
You only need to take back the gaze which you have sent forth onto an object and return it to yourself: the mysterious universal emotions will fluctuate and change upon you. You will obtain a certain kind of realization. You will "resonate" with the universe. Such a result comes from eliminating the sense of boundary between the subjective and the objective.

It is something like meditation, but it is not contemplative meditation.

You and the universe fluctuate with one another without quieting. The world, which you have always wanted to discover, is your undiscovered self.

The universe murmurs ceaselessly within you: "Humans have no 'bounds'."

"I am always with you; I have never left you. You need only to look behind you, and you will immediately sense me."

From the numerous kinds of emotions you sense "transcendent emotion" and "non-emotion."

And you go from "entering" to "exiting." Then all the waves are stilled.

It is a deathlike state, like a dead sea without waves.

The world shows again its original face.

The unification of all things is not "equality." Each thing has its own "emotional character," which appears and senses with its own strengths and weaknesses. The difference of emotion from its relative antithesis exists in the universality which includes all things.

The "emotion" of a thing is relative, abstract, and antithetical. Given the existence of this emotion, then there is the existence of that emotion. It is just as the existence of day means there must be night.

Pairs of opposites melt into the same thing.

It is like the two sides of a curtain or the two ends of a line.

We know the world, not with our brains, but with our spirits. The world is not "known" by rational, logical reasoning; instead, it appears in the mutual, mysterious sensations of non-emotional "emotions."
The "universal concepts" in our brains do not come close to the essence of the universe.
But the "universal emotions," transcendently sensed by our spirits, do.

You must "enter" and "participate" in them. The world does not stand apart from you. The invisible "stone veil," which has stood for thousands of years separating you from the world, cutting you off from the world by drawing distinctions between the subjective and the objective, the observer and the observed, the expresser and the expressed, must be "pierced," shattered.
Until this happens, the world, which has been "drawn and quartered" by concepts, can only be summarized in one word: "a misconception."

It does not matter how many spiritual concepts we create. We cannot capture the world, nor can we sense ourselves. Our lives are so meaningless; they are insufferably boring. We can only obtain "liberation" from human life through "emotions," receiving a kind of existential "release." Because emotions are directly connected to our bodies, our spirits enter into contact relations. The things which we have sensed directly, both physiologically and psychologically, are always truer, richer,

livelier, and closer to the ungraspable people and worlds than the things we believe we "know" conceptually.
Concepts are not "people," nor are they the world.
They are merely distant, restricted approximations of people and the world. "Emotions" saturate people directly, causing a direct sense of the world. From this sense, we discover that people and the world, which have been divided by our concepts, are one entity that cannot be divided. The mutual relationship between people and the universe is a self-consistent "circle." The appearance of humans is a "universal event" that never ends.

Emotional philosophy emphasizes "holistic human experiences" based on psychology and physiology; it is not the cerebral knowledge of certain abstract concepts.

Emotional philosophy is the "holistic human experience."

Universal emotions are the development and spreading of "human bodily experiences." Do we not sense that, mysteriously, a certain distant star in the universe resonates with a certain cell in our body?

"Universal emotion" is the unlimited expansion of experiencing the human body.
The universe is the enlargement of the human body. The human body is a miniature of the universe.

Emotional philosophy is the "atavistic awareness" of ancient Eastern philosophy.
It emphasizes "holistic experience" based on psychology and physiology.
It is not a kind of general "knowledge," but rather, a kind of special "sensing."
It is not a "concept," but an "emotion."
It is not secreted from the brain; but rather, it surges from the spirit and heart.

It is does not separate humans from the world; instead, it heals the "circle" of the world and humanity.

To explain humanity, one must transcend the impossible, myriad, latent things behind it.
"Humanity" is always a riddle to humans. This riddle continues without it, but it can stop temporarily.
Death is when the answer to the riddle "up to this point" is revealed.

Who among you has experienced the death of emotions when someone leaves the world forever?
No one.
Emotions include experiencing death.
Such an experience melts the unmeltable line between life and death; moreover, it stirs up the rhythm of the appearance and disappearance of life and death. When emotions spread throughout the entire human body, our sense of

sight is unable to look within to see the mysterious universal dance. All our creations (poetry, music, paintings, science, technology, etc.) are simulations of this dance. The more a person is endowed with creativity, the more he is able to approach debauchery and to sense the prehistoric, universal, vast image of this dance.

Humanity alone cannot be explained.
Human nature is not determined by itself; rather, it is determined by the nature of the entire universe connected to human nature.

Humanity is not a detail of the universe.

The people "here" cannot leave the distant, independently existing universe "there." "Here" and "there" interpenetrate each other as one.

There is no here and there.
There is no "this" and "that."

Life and death are as one.
Motion and stillness are as one.
Being and non-being are as one.
Heaven and earth are as one.
Day and night are as one.
Male and female are as one.
Inside and outside are as one.

Sensation disappears sensation.
Form disappears form.

The silence of the "Buddha" is sublime.
The stillness of emotions is "chaotic motion."

It is not enlightenment. It is not the meaning of Zen.
Behold! The body of "non-being" manifests an unending stream of humanity.
It manifests an unending stream of "non-being."
It cannot be named. It cannot be told.
There is only emotion.

First draft 1981
Second draft March 24, 1986 at night

THE SUN OF FLESH
--Modern "Poetics" II

You stare at yourself face-to-face. Eternity is like gazing.
Behold! Is that you? That nascent sun! That naked silence! That universe of trembling flesh! Is that not you?
Turn your head back and look! All of human "culture," "theory," and "systems" expose an unprecedented absurdity! The sun looks false!
The silent "non-theoretical" listens carefully to the deep implications of the flesh.
It continues listening like that. It listens without form or image.

Behold! This prehistoric globe of flesh! This prehistoric world of flesh! Apart from the prehistoric original flesh, there is no "beauty"! There is no "form," not even "poetry"!

All things are suddenly discovered far from the human body.

All things have been discovered for the first time to have no weight or the slightest significance for "existence"!
Only the prehistoric flesh is beautiful! There is only the form of prehistoric flesh! There is only the prehistoric poem of the flesh!
Hence, you should learn to cast aside that amateurish pursuit of "form," which is the trivial skill of carving insects!
Hence, you should tear to shreds the "web of cultural concepts" that ensnares you.

Living creation is only found in the "shooting forth of the original lust" of emotions!

All creative spirit is form itself!
The rich, original lust of life spills over from "poetry"!
There is no "form" that can contain it!
There is no "system" that can encompass it!
There is only the "emotion" of life shooting forth and of uncontrollable, original lusts.

The entire human body implies myriad mysterious images! The human body is the "non-conceptual" universe of sexual desire! The human body is the "unsystematic" universe of emotions!

The sun of vast naked flesh, the universe of trembling muscles, gazes face-to-face with the nascent silence. In the gaze of silence, which is as one with eternity, it finally attains to transcending "conceptual culture" and abandons it eternally.

November 9, 1986 at night

HEIDEGGER IN A "POT"
--Modern Poetics III

"Who can solve the mystery? Who understands the truth?" Heidegger jumped out saying, "Me."

He pointed out: Kant thinks we should prove there is a "world," from which the existing world is independent and separate. Kant said: This exists in me purely, but the consciousness regulated by experience proves that in space apart from me exists another.

Heidegger said: Kant called the fact that no one had ever proved "the existence of things apart from us" beyond a shadow of a doubt, "the shame of philosophy and all humanity."

Then Heidegger came forth to take it upon himself to wash away this shame from the history of human intelligence.

Heidegger believed that if we properly understand existence, it defies such proof because, in its existence, it already is that thing, and later the proofs come, thinking they must add reasoning.

The pre-existence of the outside world and its provability, in this significance, raise a "practical" question, which is impossible. Heidegger said that this is not because the result of this question leads to a Gordian knot, but because the existence of the main character in this question seems to reject the raising of the question. That which is awaiting proof is not whether "the outside world" exists and how it exists. Heidegger believes that the proposition awaiting proof is why its "worldly existence" has such a tendency; in other words, present "theories of knowledge" bury "the outside world" in nothingness, and then they come to prove its existence. Heidegger believes that the reason this happens is due to the "perishing of being." Because of this perishing, the understanding of original existence becomes the understanding of present existence. He said that if one raises "critical" questions about this kind of existentialism, one discovers that the "first and only present thing" is just a purely "inner thing."

Heidegger believes that it does not matter whether the proof of the reality of the outside world is complete or not because all such proofs make as *a priori* the ungraspable topics of whether there was a world in the beginning or whether one has a world. The root of these topics must ensure that one has a world. Therefore, "*dasein*" from the outset is relegated to viewpoint, conjecture, belief, and faith, which is to say that it is relegated to a kind of action, and this action itself is a derivative form of the existence of the "world."
Hence, Heidegger ceases speaking. Different schools of knowledge "did not just lose their way in the theories of knowledge," but also they delayed "analysis of the existence of being." Therefore, they still have not authoritatively raised the form of even the most basic questions.

This raised the philosophical question: What is the first step of the "basis" of "reality in sensory perception"?

Heidegger began to seek.
Heidegger deprived previous philosophy of all its "traditional content," and he exchanged it for a set of more worldly "nearly existing" material added to his "poetic philosophy." And he used a set of very complicated and "worldly close" or "revealed" existing worldly language. One main target of his attacks was to break down the separation between "phenomenon" and "noumenon." He broke through millennia of shades of understanding about "existence."
His "breakthrough" was that he "discovered" a *dasein* in it. After he continued Kant's "suspension of philosophy," Heidegger philosophized about "suspension of emotions."
Kant said that no one has existentially analyzed the subject as the subject in an *a priori* manner.
Heidegger "discovered" Kant's suspension—the essential suspension of present existentialism.
He thought that Kant's suspension was "caused because Kant continued the existentialist premises of Descartes."

The philosophy of human life was truly rationally and coldly suspended by Kant in the "den."
But existentialists, including the earliest ancestor Heidegger, neglected or failed to discover that the true meaning of human philosophy is not "conceptual philosophy" itself.

Kant inherited the philosophical method of Descartes, "I think therefore I am" as the existential basis. Heidegger believed that Descartes had not clearly determined "the existentialist method of thinking objects," or the existential significance of "I am." His work is to "clear up" the basis for existentialist theory, "I think therefore I am," that had not been stated clearly before. And so he revealed the necessary suspension of Descartes' existential question. He thought that it was absolutely "correct" that Descartes believed himself to "think," but Heidegger rejected "the existential significance of this existing one."

When Heidegger "cleared up" Kant, he was surprised and happy to discover "*dasein*" from a new angle in the field of philosophy.
The present means the existence of humans, who are "speaking animals."
Because Heidegger thought that existence is only the existence of the one existing, then one must express existence by first revealing the self of the one who exists. "Existence cannot be defined by the one existing. For anyone who exists, existence has always been a transcendent thing." "Existence cannot be explained by the one existing; it is really only possible in the realm of existence."

Heidegger used prolix, repetitive, and complex philosophical discourse to cover up "humanity," especially humans as "emotional animals." This philosopher has been crowned "the great teacher of poetic philosophy." His philosophy, especially his method of philosophical expression cannot yet be put into verse. It lacks the lyrical. The most important thing is that from the beginning, he made it clear that his philosophy was essentially different from traditional philosophy. An essential difference is still a kind of conceptual philosophy that has not been put into verse, but is expressed in conceptual pictures. "Man" in his philosophy (the present man) is also a kind of conceptual man. Such a man does not transmit any essential feelings to us. Heidegger used his thinking and concepts to "organize" the world. He stuffed "man" into this kind of renewed concept and not into poetical emotions of life, as he organized the philosophy of the world; he crammed man into it, and he exchanged it with the "world," which had filled previous philosophies. He exchanged the content of the "filling," but he did not exchange the essence. His philosophy seems, on the surface, to have "strange thoughts, weird concepts." In reality, it has a concept of life, word games, complex style, lengthiness, and rigidity. It purports to be a kind of "poetic philosophy," "a philosophy of irrationalism," but it is better to say it is a "modernist philosophy" like some "modern poems." He only studies the traditional philosophy of the outer world, and apart from this, he re-discovers "*dasein*" and pulls his philosophical thinking closer to humans. He goes through all the concepts related to existence (in reality he just covers language and concepts), and subjects them to a new "rational interpretation." His manner of thinking and expressing is just a kind of rationally colored, highly concentrated scolding.

When the film of Heidegger's "irrationalist" philosophy is "developed," it is covered with veins and capillaries of reason. For millennia, beginning with the ancient Greeks—Socrates, Aristotle, and Plato—cultural consciousness and rational thought have spread to the present, and their shadows saturate his work. It does not matter how much he tries to escape from the shackles of traditional ways of philosophical thinking. He strives to make his philosophy come near to poetry, humanity, and life, but life is not a dead "den," nor is it an absolute, shriveled thought. It is not in human concepts. Life is in itself. Only poetry can touch it. The true poetic philosophy is the only thing that can approach life. Heidegger is far from poetry. He is not a philosopher-poet, nor is he a poet-philosopher. He used the sharp teeth of philosophy to chew up the true, red meat of life. His philosophy cannot escape swallowing the logic, rational interpretation, reasoning, and categorization of life; it is limited by these unpoetic procedures or methods. He cannot escape the trap of fraudulent concepts made by human cunning. When we pull open the nagging dross of his words, we discover that Heidegger is the same as his forerunner Kant, in that he is sitting formally in his den engaging in shriveled thinking. He is just a philosophical spider entrapping himself in the myriad convolutions of a "conceptual" spider web.

What is existence? It is not a definition. It is not a linguistic structure to be grasped; rather, it is the direct emotion of an unregulated life.

"Existence" deeply hides apart from rational "understanding." We can only "sense" it from philosophical emotions.

Philosophical emotions have broadened the distance between philosophy and traditional rational philosophy; it is a psychological divide, which rational thought cannot cross.

Heidegger "cleared" "*dasein*" out of Kant. We sense, discover, and pull out "emotions" that were hidden in Heidegger's own language and conceptual scum.

The separating barrier of concepts made the great poetic philosopher, Heidegger, unable to sense his poetical existence.
And this separating barrier of concepts made him unable to sense that he had discovered the essence of "*dasein*," which is just to exist poetically as an "individual living universal emotion."
When Heidegger suggested the great suspension of Kant's philosophy, he also created an "emotional suspension" of poetic, living philosophy.
Philosophical concepts collapse into philosophical concepts.

What is Heidegger?
—A great master who created his own living, hard philosophical language!
—A philosophical fool who played word games using language with burdensome connotations!
—A "troublesome" world piled up and wrongly placed

from a redundant, complicated, chaotic, and disconnected conceptual system!

—A "troublesome" philosopher!

Heidegger's vocabulary is very dry. His language constructs a kind of deeply concealed awkwardness and artificiality that has not yet been revealed to the world.

Shouting is a kind of silence. Conversation never puts on voices. Shouts come from homeless, voiceless, and breathless ones. Their plight is essentially closed to normal people.

I have greatly, hugely simplified these words, but Heidegger rambles on in countless long, boring essays. The world of his "poetic philosophy" greatly lacks poetry. The poetic language of his philosophy stubbornly resists the rich, simple clarity of the language of poetry.

"We have called the end of a living thing the conclusion. *Dasein* is very similar to any living thing in its physiological death. Even though such death is not the annihilation of death in the existential state or in its original existence, it participates in regulation through this form of existence. *Dasein* can be ended without actually dying; however, as *dasein*, it is not simply the conclusion. Since this is the case, we call such situations "decease." And death is the term used by *dasein* to refer to its death in an existential form. Hence, this means that *dasein* is never-ending. But *dasein* can only be deceased at the time of its death."

You see how much Heidegger likes to use these ways of thinking and words that wind around and around trying to say everything, while saying nothing clearly!
Moreover, Heidegger is forced to create some terms, like "trouble," "world as world," "state of instantly doing," "state of doing," "*dasein*," and "suspension." He stuffs the world into them, forcing himself and others to believe that these concepts were discovered in the world.

One who exists in the world has always developed with the present world.

Death is merely a kind of existential stage, the existence that only exists in approaching death.

The existence of "*dasein*" is troublesome.

Heidegger had so much philosophical color in his language! His words are not poetical, nor are they of life, nor are they true. Heidegger believed that existence is the existence of the one existing. Although philosophy does not study the one existing but existence itself, there is no way to contact existence itself apart from the one existing. In order to touch existence, one must seek out such an existing one, whose essence is "to exist."

In the end, he exhausts his mind in discovering that the one existing is "*dasein*."
When Heidegger was expressing his philosophy, I suspect that his thinking was influenced by Eastern philosophy, especially Zen Buddhism, and the style of his language is still that incomprehensible, gloomy language.

He said *dasein* does not exist "here" or "there"; rather, it exists in itself.

This means that *dasein* brings its "existence" wherever it is. And since *dasein* is not "here," nor is it "there," it makes "here" or "there" into possible premises.
Therefore, *dasein* "exists here" and "existence is here." It expresses the "manifestation" or "understanding" of a kind of Heideggerian conceptual state.

Dasein is *dasein* because it has some sort of action towards its existence. Human existence is survival.
He adds the analysis of the theory of survival onto the existence of *dasein* to form the premise and basis for all other existential analysis. Hence, this analysis is also called the theory of basic analysis.
Existentialism is also phenomenology.
The phenomenology of *dasein* is hermeneutics.
The level on which the prevalent and formal phenomenological concept engages in study is called "phenomenal."

And the level on which the phenomenological concept of phenomenology engages in study is called "phenomenological."

Dasein exists daily in a state of "being darkly covered." The dark covering is of two kinds: one is the dark covering over the state of the one existing, which is a state of being veiled; the other is an existential dark covering, which is a state of being sealed up.

Dasein is a matter of "removing the dark coverings" to arrive at the realm of uncovered "reality" or "truth."

There are two similar significances to the dark covering. The uncovered truth includes both the significance of the truth of existence and of the truth of the existing one. And the former is in the first position, or the "developed state," "developed"; the latter is in the second position, or "the state of being revealed."

Moving towards the truth is the development of existence. Development manifests itself when *dasein* is "understood" in the world.

The existence of *dasein* is "in the world."
The essence of *dasein* in the world is "vexation."
Vexation should be grasped from its vexing variety of different meanings. First, there is the "vexation" in the theory of survival, and then there is the "vexation" in psychology.

Vexation is a kind of "apparent emotional state," which possesses a kind of impetus to "reveal itself." This impetus is to "stand up," to "understand."

"Understanding" itself is the "planning and preparation" for possibility.

The basic method of "planning and preparation" is to explain things.

"Explanation" is carried out by "speaking."

The "state of self-revelation" and "understanding" are realized through "speaking," and move towards "destruction."

Dasein exists in the world essentially as "vexation." And the total construction of the three basic stages of "vexation"—"understanding," "self-revelation," and "destruction," with their three true and false states—are illuminated over time. Existence itself is developed in time. Heidegger calls the time in which existence develops the "horizon" or "vision."

The time which is the realm of "vexation" includes the three links of "past," "future," and "present," and they possess two kinds of states: true and false.

Time is constantly "arriving." Heidegger calls this attribute of time "leaving itself," or "breaking out." This characteristic of time determines that the process of *dasein's* existence in the world is a creative process of constantly "leaving itself," constantly "breaking out." As time constantly "leaves itself," it "arrives," and this characteristic causes the existence of *dasein* in the world to become "history"... The preceding is a simple recounting of Heidegger's system of thought.

Heidegger tears down his predecessors' conceptual frameworks, And on the old ground of philosophy, he builds "Heidegger's framework."

But the world has not come closer to us because of his "system" because the world is not a "Heideggerian construct"; life did not become more approachable to us because he completed his philosophy, since life cannot be brought into a "Heideggerian mold."

It does not matter if these "constructs" and "molds" exchange their conceptual materials or are called by someone else's name. Their forms, their styles, and their frameworks still come from the same blueprint as that of the past; they use the same methods of expression.

They still are "concept" after "concept", "framework" after "framework."

Heidegger writes long litanies in which he never gets bored of narrating concept after concept, and they all wrap around this one word: *dasein*. He merely defines how "only those existing ones who at every time and in every place perform some actions for their own existence can be said to have attained *dasein*." This is to say that in his concept *dasein* refers to "humans." It refers to human conceptual existence and not to the status of one who conceptually exists. *Dasein* always confirms oneself, and the actions confirming *dasein* are things apart from what is confirmed. This is what Heidegger means when he speaks of the preeminence of "going to exist" and "going to be" with respect to "essence," "what it is," and "being."

The difference between Heidegger's philosophy and that of his predecessors is merely that he exchanges for *dasein*

Hegel's "reason" or "absolute spirit," Kant's "self-existing object," the "will to life" which Schopenhauer and Nietzsche separately affirmed or denied. The mold of Heidegger's thinking and the language he uses to express himself still do not escape from the stereotypes of past philosophers and the system of philosophy that has existed for thousands of years. And in the matter of lyrically expressing himself in a poetic philosophy, his realm, language, passion, and imagery are actually lower than those of Nietzsche. With respect to the "poetic" significance of "poetic philosophy," Heidegger, coming after Nietzsche, represents a reversal in the matter of "emotion" in the philosophy of life.

On the ruins of the razed philosophical concepts of his predecessors, he rebuilds his own conceptual philosophy, and the moment this philosophy faces the poetry of the reality of life, it certainly cannot escape its ultimate destiny of self-destruction! Heidegger's philosophy is far from the "poetry" of "poetic philosophy," and far from the life in "philosophy of life."

Its fatal weakness is that it lacks both life and poetry.

Its conceptual "system" that was to last for thousands of years will come crashing down, and then it will have collapsed into a pile of new "conceptual ruins."

The brightly shining light of "genius guessing"

Heidegger has touched upon emotions.
I am referring to "emotions" in the philosophical sense and not in the psychological sense.

He says: "*dasein*—as the emotional state of present being," "when existentialism refers to present being, it refers to the state which the one who exists knows best, the most ordinary thing: emotions, having emotions."

"Emotional philosophy" or the emotions of poetic life philosophy begin to shine brightly in Heidegger's "genius guessing," in which he unconsciously finds the beginning. But he has no way to open up the myriad, ever-changing emotional illusions and pass through the human body to the mystery of universal emotions. He is a very logical person. He uses his logic to frame the world. The only difference between him and the philosophers who preceded him is that he changes the contents of the frame: "Heideggerian framework" or "Heideggerian concepts." Heidegger undoubtedly lacks a sense of mystery. He refuses such things. Mystery is not mystery. It is only the very ordinary world that has always been like this, but which our intelligence has not yet penetrated to comprehend. Heidegger seems to have received some inspiration from Eastern philosophy and religions, but he did not explore the depths of the bottomless mysteries of universal emotions in the human body because they are something that purely rational analysis and logical determinations cannot touch. Nor can the pure reason, which we usually train, sense or "understand" them. They are the primitive Eastern mysteries, and they are a normal spiritual state. They "resonate" at the subconscious level with the emotional sense of a modern human philosophy of life. It escapes the frame of a gigantic conceptual system. It

melts away fixed conceptual frameworks. It externalizes and spreads in the "poetry" of life.
Philosophy, spiritual philosophy, is not in the gray matter of the brain. Its spirit is not in the marvelous map of the brain.

Philosophy of life belongs to the spirit, to the unadorned spirit.

It is the philosophy of "the universal emotions of the human body."

Heidegger said that people are accustomed to seeing knowledge as "a relationship between the subjective and the objective," but the "truth" included in this view is empty. The subjective and the objective like *dasein* and the world are not differentiated, but united.
It does not matter if it is the differentiated subjective and objective or the united *dasein* and the world, both are not of the spirit, not of the senses, not of a true conceptual state. Their "truth" (if indeed they can contain "truth") is also empty. Here there are only the life emotions of philosophy, the universal emotions of the human body. Such "emotions" refer to the reality of life, which is truly a poetic life that mutually includes the significance of human and world philosophy, which is "circularly self-consistent."
Although Heidegger touches on "emotions," he neglects **the universal nature of the emotions of the human body**. He locks them up with the dry concept of *dasein*.
Heidegger proposes that the first systematic definition of emotions be given within the framework of psychology, but rather,

its earliest systematic explanation was in Aristotle's *Rhetoric*. The Stoics also defined emotions.

Heidegger believes: "Since the time when Aristotle expounded the general principles of the existence of emotions, there has been almost no progress worth noting. The situation is exactly the opposite: All kinds of emotions have been studied and classified as psychological phenomena. They are usually ranked together with ideas and desires as psychological phenomena with tertiary functions. They have been demoted to epiphenomena."

This is truly the insight of a genius!

But this is as far as Heidegger gets! He does not continue moving towards "emotions" to set one foot outside of determinism! His linear intellect and knowledge hinder him! His *dasein* raises a vague and invisible screen that makes him unable to pierce through life or to leap over life to make a "completely emotional" philosophical overview of universal life. His mastery of "poetic philosophy" lacks the poetic angle. He sees "emotions," but he cannot touch the breath and blood of emotional life. Nevertheless, it is hard for him in the purely logical meditations of his writings to elevate "emotions to the most essential heights of "poetry," or to plumb the depths of "poetic philosophy," or to dig out the philosophical origins of the "universal emotions" of life.

He can only consider this as "the existence of one who exists."

Faced with the possibility of a revolutionary change in philosophical consciousness, Heidegger once raised this series of questions:

"Should we, perhaps, make a detailed inquiry into the ontological significance of actual things and conceptual things?"
"I have heard that **there really is such a relationship**."
"What is it that prevents the rationality of this question? For two thousand years, this quesiton has not made the slightest progress. Is it by chance? Is it because before we begin, the question has already been skewed, and the question concerning the ontological significance of actual things and conceptual things has been skewed?"

But Heidegger's inquiries only "go so far," as well.
He has no way to escape the bonds of traditional philosophical discourse, which confine him.
Regardless of how much he repudiates tradition, the skeleton of his philosophy is still rational.
Regardless of how much he tries to make life poetic, his philosophy only skews life and is skewed by life.
This is a conceptual criticism of the "conceptual philolosophy" conceived by one who went before.
To Heidegger, the living world is not flesh and blood or actual or seamless; rather, it is chopped up into complex and chaotic concepts. The face of "poetry" does not exist anywhere.
In this sense, Heidegger's "poetic philosophy" exhibits "shallowness in its depths" and is "deeply shallow."

His entire conceptual framework is merely an interlocking pile of conceptual bricks laid without mortar.
Its tight structure is essentially loose.
It cannot withstand the slightest blow from life!
If we say that Kantian philosophy had certain "philosophical lapses," then Heidegger's philosophy is an "emotional lapse" of "poetic philosophy."
Even today, philosophy can no longer be borne by "philosophy"!

Philosophy, as a kind of "philosophy," has a systematic form that is already futile formalism.
The quantity of its flow of magnificent thought has decreased; the level of its waters has gone down; its flowing waters are facing a dangerous blockage!
It has hoarded a pile of concepts that have become sludge, a mudslide.
It has lost its power to move, its power to motivate! The boat of life is no longer able to navigate its waters!
It should seek to open the sluice gates of philisophical pithiness outside the complex "system" that has already been constructed. It should return "poetic philosophy" to the "poetry" of life, and it should return "universal emotions" to the human body.
Yes, for the past few millennia, this world has been piled high with "systems."
Each system is a grand concept; buried within each great concept lies a hidden, great illusion.
The consciousness of life should awaken and come out of the illusions of philosophy.

A Reactionary Life and World: Humanity is "Poetry"

When Heidegger rejected the ontologies of all kinds of metaphysics from traditional philosophy, he thought he had discovered a new ontology with transcendent significance. He forced upon us the discovery of an immutable word: "*dasein*," and he placed it between "existence and time." We know that his *dasein* refers to humans, and according to his explanation, humans "live poetically upon this earth." But "humanity" in existentialim is not the humanity expressed conceptually; rather, it is humanity existing emotionally. He says that humans are the poetic "inhabitants" of this world. It would be better to say that they are simply "poetry." From the angle of life itself (not as a state of human existence), humans are like the music of poetry, like the painting of poems. They are the form of solidified music, the flowing scenes of a painting. Humans exhibit themselves, react to themselves, and listen to themselves.

When humans react to themselves, they must "react" emotionally, using all the senses of life.

When humans react emotionally to themselves, they are reacting to the world around them. They react and listen to the earth, the seas, and the heavenly bodies.

Humanity is poetry.

Humans react to the world and to themselves.

"React" here includes all the senses of sight, hearing, touch, smell, and taste.

Humans react to their "colors," to their energies, to their melodies, to their compositions, to their expressions, to their sculptures, to their voices, to their feelings, to their flesh and blood, and to their emotional philosophies. These emotional philosophies flow through the entire human body and must be "heard" with the entire human body.

Humanity is a poem that speaks silently, without written language;
A painting daubed with emptiness, without colors;
A heavenly melody, played without instruments;
A statue that captures time and space, without traces of having been carved;
A theatrical production that explains life, without a script.

Humans fill up and enrich the empty spaces of the world, naturally, without artificiality.
They themselves are a work of living philosophy of humans reacting to themselves.
They gather together all forms of artistic expression into one; they contain in themselves all forms of expression.
They exhibit in being exhibited.
They mold in being molded.
They are the creators of all art.

And they are all the mysterious "readers."

Heidegger's "Pot"

Heidegger formulated a philosophical "pot."

It is stored in the chapter on "The Thing" in his book *Poetry, Language, and Thought*.
It is the "pot" of *dasein*.
When I gaze at Heidegger's water pot, I discover that it is weak. It hides from my questioning gaze, shrinking back. It is unable to "show" itself, nor does it dare to.
Heidegger only gives us a lifeless vessel.
It is not existence itself.
His "water pot" is a withered "pot of meditation."
His representation of the pot is merely a kind of still life, a description of the entire static web of connections to that still life.
He is never able to transmit to us the "dynamics" of that still life or the dynamic process of its reality.

The "pot" is represented to us, but it does not appear;

It is transmitted to us without ever reaching us;
It draws our gaze without ever entering our line of sight;

It makes our thoughts abstract, but it has no way to touch our nervous system, to shake us with sensory stimulation.

Its "quality" is much less than that of a poem; like the "whale dream" (see "World, Your Exposed Body and Your Hidden Body"), it has value as a message.

Heidegger, who is exhausted in his thoughts and strength, only gives us a dried up, empty conceptual pot.

Even the "emptiness" of this "pot" does not convey a nuanced concept.
Although Heidegger gives us a water pot, our spirits are unable to use it for drinking.
Heidegger's "pot" reveals that Heidegger's "*dasein*" is a "philosophical" existence, a "conceptual" existence, a "bookish" existence, an existence of the "human brain."

The root of his "irrational" philosophy is not poetry.
It is not the "universal" existence that thrives in the world of the human body, the existence of the life of flesh and blood. His "*dasein*" is shriveled, just as his philosophical "pot" is shrunken.

Heidegger's philosophical "pot" is not textured; his "*dasein*" is not sexual, flexible, or sensory.
He only uses words to draw a subjective "human" for us.

It is a human without a nervous system.

Such a "human" does not breathe, does not communicate. When the "poetic philosopher" Heidegger forcibly stuffed "*dasein*" into "existence," he also forced upon us a "non-poetic" or not-truly-poetic "philosophical pot." He was unable to pass it out of philosophy. He was unable to pass it into our hands. It was merely a written form of "soldering." Heidegger was unable to "remove it" from the written word.

Unless we "smash" the written words in the transcendent realm of the written word, we are unable to sense its "non-conceptual" existence.

Heidegger was trapped in the realm of the conceptual world.

His "poetic philosophy" is only a conceptual expression, lacking "poetic" expression, lacking "poetry."

This is Heidegger's difficulty.

It is the dual-difficulty of non-poetic, philosophical thought and non-poetic language.

Heidegger's "philosophical thought" cannot be broken, nor can it hold water, neither can it slake a certain level of spiritual, existential "thirst" for us.

This pot is a piece of unworked pottery that has not been fired, painted, or glazed.

A conceptual "pot."

Even if Heidegger's "poetic philosophy" were to exchange its "contents," from the angle of philosophical "poetics," his form of thought and apparent language do not truly, completely transcend his predecessors.

His irrational philosophy is still rational.
The form of his thought and language is still "classical."

Heidegger's philosophical, conceptual pot only has the non-abstract ability to convey to us abstractions.
Only the ability to smash a philosophical pot enables it to arrive at the level of an "unbreakable" philosophical pot.

Only a "pot" that can hold water is able to rise to the ultimate limit of being a pot without water; it is "empty" in the sense of being filled with water and not quenching the eternally unquenchable thirst of the spirit of humanity.

Heidegger's empty philosophical pot is merely the "pot" of empty philosophy. If we use the angle of "poetics" for comparing it to the "emptiness" in the poem of the "whale's dream," a poem "without a drop of water" in the "empty cave of the whale's dream," then the latter poem gives human philosophy the tactile sense of being "poetic" in its inutterable, mysterious message and its immeasurable spiritual depths.
Poetic philosophy must "meld" poetry into it.
And a philosophy of poetry or the poeticization of philosohpy is absolutely not "an idea."

At this point, we have now completely discovered that Heidegger had imprisoned himself in Heidegger's philosophical "pot," which he fashioned from his concepts.

If we want to touch existence, we must smash this "pot" and rescue Heidegger and philosophy out from the "pot."

The world is in the "non-pot."

Now and only now, our philosophical "listening" can arrive at the level of an empty "pot."

Non-Poetic Speaking: Heidegger's Language

Heidegger said that greatness is found where poetry determines the person and name of the poet.
So, the "poetry" exhibited in all of the poetic philosopher Heidegger's philosophy, from another angle, also determines his person and name as a "poetic philosopher."
Heidegger expressed doubt that the "conceptual bonds of language can be broken," but he never broke them. He was still tied up in expressing himself in the "linguistic concept" of purely conceptual language. He intended to make his philosophy "poetic," but he could not "speak" in poetry.
Heidegger said, "Language speaks. People only speak during the time when they hear the call of language and answer that call. In the matter of our human existence, which can come out from ourselves and together with ourselves becomes the entire call of speaking, language is the highest. Language calls us, first but again at the last, moving towards the nature of the matter." "When people listen truly to the call of language in their answer, they use the essence of poetry to

speak. The more lyrical the poet—the freer his speaking—the more purely he is forced to endeavor to listen constantly and the more his speech transcends simple statements. With respect to the judgment of this statement, people only discern its accuracy or error."

Heidegger's language is actually the kind of language that he said is not free—"speaking" without the element of poetry. We have no way to "listen" with our spirits and thus answer the call of his philosophy. His language is just a kind of "simple statements," and faced with this kind of rational statement, we can only use "reason" to judge whether it is "correct" or "erroneous."
That is all.
Where is the poetry? The poetry or "the lyrical" is too far from this kind of language.
Poetry transcends "rational statements."
Because it is full in its own nature, it also transcends judgments of whether it is "correct" or "erroneous."
Because this is the case, Heidegger has no way to strongly prove by his "speaking" with language why "thought" and "poetry" both belong to existence. Nor can he use language to "say" why the manifestation of self exists in the self "that has poetry," why the real language of thought is "poetry," and what is "true speaking." Even if "poetic language really is the true speaking," Heidegger cannot prove or demonstrate this with his language itself.

Because the language of this master of poetic philosophy, the originator of existentialism, is simply the linguistic form of expression, synopsis, transmission, accounting, and explanation, his "poetics" are stuck onto it, and its nature is not "poetic."

Heidegger's "language" speaks in "non-speaking."
"Non-speaking" here does not refer to the deeply silent non-speaking that transcends speech; rather, it refers to the non-speaking, which does not contain "poetry."
His speaking remains in ceaselessness; it is speech that patiently has not stopped.
He teaches us to listen carefully to what is purely said in poetry, but his language is not strong enough to exhibit the "pure speech" of poetry.
Heidegger's language is a language that has never had the sun shine upon it;
It is language that has never been washed by the waves;

It is language that does not show us branches or spreading grass roots;

It is language that does not shiver when the wind blows;

It is language without the silhouette of a house;
It is language without the shiny fur and breath of beasts;
It is language without the nerves of plants;
It is language without the vision of insects;

It is language that is unable to fall into the womb of the universe to nose around;
It is language that cannot arrive at the darkness and cannot reach the light;
It is language that is not the movement of stars or the stars moving.

It is the dead language stripped from the human body.
It is not "spoken" poetry, nor is it "poetic" speaking.
Spoken "poetry" is poetic "non-speaking."
Poetic language is the language of "silence" and language "without words."
In poetry, language disappears from the "flow of language"; life begins from the place where "the flow of language is lost."
Poetry constructed by words is apart from its linguistic construction; it is apart from the structure of language.
Life, which is sprouting full of semantics and words, is a wasteland of life; life is without the encumbrance of semantics and words. It is naked and blank. And such "blankness" is really a rich emptiness. The ability to read and comprehend "emptiness" is also the ability to read and comprehend life.
Poetic language adds strength to "blankness"; it opens up "blankness." It returns life to the simplicity and purity of a blank sheet of paper, and it clears a broad, limitless space for life.
Poetry packed with "language" crowds out life; this is the loss of the life of language.
Poetry that has purposely "structured language" assem-

bles and structures life, closing up life in the "assemblage" of language.
Poetry that specializes in "polished" language vainly adorns life, suffocating life in decorative packaging.
Poetry that pretends with "experimental language" "stylizes" life, mummifying life and making poetry into an artifact or literary object that can be "excavated" and researched.
Poetic language is not "language" itself. It bears the message of life and strongly "rejects" purely instrumental language.

Life is definitely not a "linguistic experiment," even though it does borrow its expression from spoken and written language.
Poetry that is saturated with life transcends language.
It is not separated from life by a pile of linguistic bricks.

A pile of linguistic bricks insulates poetry from life.
Life in poetry is not a "work of assembling language." The poet divines the spirit, plumbs the depths of unknown worlds, but he is not a "professional technocrat of language." Poetry completes the "silences" and the "wordlessness" of language.
Intelligence is the highest expression and the highest level of "silence" and "wordlessness."

The language of poetry is a kind of mistiness, like a light far away in the fog.
It has a kind of transparency like bees and tree leaves that can be seen within the translucence of amber.

It has a kind of volatility like the indefinite ripples made by wind on the water.
It has a kind of sudden onset like sudden, frightened screams in the dark night.
It has a kind of directness like an electric shock.
It has a certain loss of control that is hard to contain, like the pulsing muscles of a skinned frog.
Sometimes it is barbed like a wound, hiding unseen blades.
Sometimes it has clonic spasms of thundering deep thoughts, aggressively forcing people to retreat.

Poetry that uses linguistic expression must distance itself from the fetters of language before it can attain to the most perfect freedom. The distance from language to poetry is the measure by which poetry transcends language.
People who leave the poem itself and only pay attention to the structure and change of the language are no different from a watchmaker, who only pays attention to the structure of the watch and who only hopes to make structural changes to it. The language of poetry has itself become the indicator of how the cogs turn and the fixtures move; the poem itself has become a lifeless clock, a machine that is driven by people. The poet is merely a watchmaker, who occasionally comes to tighten the clockwork. Such clocklike poetry or mechanical poetry has no way to represent life, no matter how beautiful its structure or how delicate its assemblage! Neither can it strike the "universal hours" of life!

It is only a linguistic clock;
It is only a dead machine, mechanically moving.
And the poet is just a literary watchmaker!
Heidegger is such a watchmaker of "poetic philosophy."
His works are a "poetic" clock.

He turns the cogs and springs of language to move "abstruseness."
His philosophy has oily breath and the scars of metal teeth. The accretion of thoughts moves with difficulty. In it, we cannot see life, nor can we see the poetic footprints of the "universal emotions" of the human body.

Both the "poetic philosophy" of Watchmaker Heidegger's thoughts and the "clock" of Heidegger's philosophy should be destroyed at their foundations and have their original "structure" shattered!
The universe is a "clock" that transcends structure!
Life itself is the indicator of poetry!
The person speaking is the person himself and the "confluence of language" that exists without words, without language, without voice apart from the person.

Traditional metaphysics divides the unity of humans with the world. It considers the "existing" person to be the primary premise, and it sees objects "existing" separately as the secondary premise. Most traditional philosophy has always followed and continued this metaphysical dualism of primary and secondary premises. This did not start to end until Nietszche. Nietszche prominently represents the total collapse of traditional metaphysics and the beginning of modern poetic philosophy. Metaphysical dualism brought out the separation and conflict between poetry and existence, poetry and truth. Heidegger tried to dissolve and join together the rift between existence, truth, and poetry, in order to express the establishment of a poetic existence and truth, or he intended to have existential poetics and authentic poetics. But Heidegger did not complete such "poetic" intentions. Speaking from the angle of poetic philosophy, he only completed a narration. Faced with the union of poetry and philosophy, he lacked poetic "expression."

As an intellectual and a thinker, Heidegger saw the world as a "classroom," and he gave the world a narration of poetic thought or thoughtful poetry.

He did not make "poetry" come alive in "thought," nor did he saturate "poetry" with "thoughts." In his writings, these two things are only "stuck together." They do not attain to the mutual interpenetration or unity that he hoped for or planned.

Heidegger is merely a calm lecturer in a philosophy classroom. He is not a thoughtful poet, nor is he really a poetic thinker. He lacks poetic imagination; he is limited within a prison of thoughts and pale in his language.

With respect to cosmological significance, he is "without emotion."

Pointing from Outside the Picture: Heidegger's Points

Heidegger sees all works of art, all things in existence, in the shadow of traditional aesthetic explanations. He sees the tragedy of the long-term separation of the primary and secondary topics in the realm of aesthetics, and he tries to shake things and to transcend the dualistic conflict in aesthetics, allowing art to become "the manifestation of existence itself."

He analyzes poetry and painting for us as examples.
He points out to us that in the paintings and in the poetry "the one existing enters" its own "open existence." He shows us the "unveiled truth" that occurs in such a state.
His finger points to existence as he tells us to look at "existence."

He stands at the abstract boundary between philosophy and poetry, thinking the thought of an abstract boundary. The "existence" that he "defines" for us does not yet exist in his "conceptual realm."
He himself has not yet been "artistically manifested" to us as existence.
This is because he did not find a kind of "poetic" manner of "emotionally thinking," and he lacks the expression of "the emotional language" of "poetry."
He is only "teaching" us; however, he does not "touch" us as existence itself, nor does he "awaken" us. He has no way to "enter into" us.

When he points to "points" in this way, we only see the primary premise that is pointed out to us and the secondary premise to which it points.

He divides again with his "pointing" when he "teaches" us, creating the very division between the primary and secondary premises that he opposes.

Heidegger's concept that "art is a manifestion of existence itself" fails in his unartistic, conceptual definition.

Just as he forgets "emotions" in his philosophy, so also, in his aesthetics he forgets **emotion—universal emotions and not merely "emotion" in the significance of artistic psychology**.

As humans face all the works of art, all the existing objects, which encompass them, electric currents of life shock the "universal emotions."

It happened! The primary and secondary premises have become "one" and are simultaneously "touched" and "awakened"; they "enter into" one another, producing a unified resonance!

This does not require "teaching"! It does not require "pointing out"!

"Existence" itself is a person out of control.

This is a human radiating "universal emotions" as an "emotional animal."

Humans "touch" themselves! They "call" themselves! They "shake" themselves!

They press close to mystery. At this time, mystery reflects mystery. From it, humans discover that they themselves are mysterious.

This is truth.
When we gaze on a painting, we have not yet discovered that someone secretly accomplished an instantaneous "transfer." People open like houses. It is a "temporary lease" giving us the right of residence in the house of another person's being. Or, when we enter into the painting, we have already been pushed into a space which it is not. We are standing in the mysterious "being" pointed to by the picture.
We take back the right of residence that was "transferred."
People are no longer objects outside the painting, nor have they "become" the main premise.
They are simply the "being" whose existence is mysteriously pointed to.
All this occurs in an instant.
The painting that is independent from you accepts you in an instant.
The world is filled with "pointing." The skies are filled with "pointing." Everyone is "pointing." Everyone has something to which they "point."
Heidegger is also "pointing." He "points" to poetry; he "points" to painting. He points from outside the poetry. He points from outside the picture.

Existence points from within, not pointing.

The Misunderstanding of Metaphysics and Heidegger's Misunderstanding

Heidegger believes that the objective existence of works of art is first to establish the world.
Is this how it really is? No!
The objective existence of works of art is first and only the existence of the world itself.
The world does not need to "establish" itself, nor does it have anything with which to establish itself, and the world as a work of art is also like this. An objective work of art has already been completed; its "world" is "existing," and not "established."
As Heidegger said: "The world is not built before us, allowing us to carefully measure it as an object. Hence, birth and death, blessing and cursing, constantly cause us to enter into existence; therefore, the world is not our object."

Then, the "world" of a work of art, similarly, does not only stand before us "allowing us to carefully measure it as an object."
As a work of art, it is complete. The objective existence of the world is an independently existing world. It constantly causes us to enter into the existence of "birth and death, blessing and cursing," and that is to constantly enter into the existence of the work itself.

The world of any work is never an independent world, separate from us.
It is the existence of the world itself.

We have no way to sever this "world" from the world.
We have no way to make this "existence" separate from existence. Heidegger said that the world "has become worldly," but actually it is just that the world has been separated from his conceptual world. The world in his conceptual world is "without" world. He analyzes a picture of a pair of farmer's shoes painted by Van Gogh, and he actually thinks that there is only that farm woman "there in the open existence." (That is only his association of ideas from the farmer's shoes, and she is an invisible farm woman who only exists in his imagination.). And only from this is there "a world." Stones, plants, and animals regardless of how closely connected they are to us, regardless of our total construction of a similar world for ourselves, as soon as they are in Heidegger's conceptual world, they cannot "be opened." Hence, Heidegger has "no world" in his eyes. Heidegger has driven them out of his conceptual world.

Heidegger thinks that when a world opens, everything in it has its own speed, distance, and size; therefore, the stones, plants, and animals "without a world," that cannot be opened, are outside of Heidegger's "world." They are outside of the rhythm of time, of the perspective of space, and of all the movements of time and space in existence; therefore, they lose their own "speed, distance, and size."
Heidegger thinks he transcends the dualistic conflict of traditional metaphysics and that he establishes his aesthetics in existence itself. First he affirms: "The objective existence of

works of art is establishing the world," while simultaneously emphasizing: "The objective existence of works of art is secondary to manifesting the earth."

He thinks that the world and the earth are different but inseparable. The former opens to us, and the latter closes to us. The two stand in opposition in "a kind of conflict," as the establishment of the world and the manifestation of the earth "consent to this conflict." And the "truth" of the "unveiling" and "lack of veils" of the revelation of existence is produced by this conflict. He thinks that art produces and makes truth. The truth of aesthetics is a method of revelation.

Therefore, Heidegger's definition of aesthetics refers to "existence, which has been forgotten."

So, how and in what manner does art "reveal" through existence? How and in what manner does the objective existence of works of art "manifest" the earth?

I do not know. We only hear Heidegger's empty noise.

We do not see or hear anything about this "revelation," this "manifestation," and we have no way to sense it.

Heidegger only gives us a different conceptual system from what went before. He does not help us move forward towards a concept that escapes pure language; he does not give us anything non-conceptual that is closer to existence.

The mutually different but inseparable world and earth to him are only conceptual "opening" and "closing." The two are in "conflict," and they are only in "conflict" in his concept, and they seem to be totally unrelated to our senses.

The world is essentially a whole, but he must distinguish between the "world" and the "earth."

A work of art is essentially a whole, but he must point out that within it there exists the "conflict" between the earth and the world; as a work which "allows the conflict" between the "establishment of the world" and the "manifestation of the earth," the "truth" occurs in this conflict and "is revealed" in an "aesthetic" manner.

Heidegger steps out of the misunderstanding of the conceptual system of metaphysics, but he turns into another conceptual system where he gets lost, and he steps out in a new "misunderstanding." He falls into the deep pit of the words he creates, and he drags the world with him as he jumps down.

When he eliminates the cracks from the mutual opposition of the primary and secondary premises, he does not simultaneously bring us into "existence." Instead, he presents to us a kind of conceptual (note: it is conceptual) elimination of the "existential" split between the primary and secondary premises, but he still does not overcome the barrier raised by words. Heidegger seems to discover a "forgotten" existence, but he reburies existence in non-"poetic" words. His "*dasein*" has no way to escape from the shroud of utterly non-poetic language.

Heidegger also buries his "truth" in the tomb of words that he creates.

Such "truth" can never be the "revelation" in existence; it can never be revealed in an "aesthetic" manner in an unaesthetic, pure existence.

Heidegger merely tries to "poetify" his "conceptual existence" and make this "conceptual existence poetic."
He attempts to "make existence artistic" and "make art existential"; existential "aesthetics" and "aesthetic" existentialism.

But art is not an image of non-verbal concepts and conceptual words.

Aesthetic form does not exist within concepts, but rather in the instincts of life.
Heidegger, the non-poet, clearly exposes the fact that he is far away from "art" and "aesthetics," especially when he tries to pass through "poetry" to grasp "art" and "aesthetics."
Heidegger floats outside of "poetry." He floats outside of "the world" and "the earth." But he firmly stands in the "existence" of his conceptual world.
He never moves his standing point, nor does he doubt or question it!

He only tears down the temple of his predecessors' metaphysical philosophies, while simultaneously building for himself a "Heidegger temple" founded on his conceptual system.
Hence, all humanity discovers again that a new "Heidegger" god has been raised in the place of yesterday's idols.

Now is the time to invite the "god" out of the temple!
Heidegger is not the new "god" of modern poetic philosophy, nor is he an existential "philosopher" who lives poetically.

It is only a new "conceptual pimple," waiting for us to pop it.
It is not "lyrical"!
It is not "poetic"!
He "passes through" the process of poetic philosophy.
In the history of human philosophy, Heidegger does not really use poetic systems of thought and forms of language to break through the rational conceptual definitions of traditional philosophy and to shake the foundations of traditional philosophy, which are lazy in their existence, thus accomplishing a great turn in poetic philosophy.
Poetic philosophy had a "all-encompassing" accomplishment in Nietzsche! Heidegger's philosophy does not accomplish a new transcendence in "poetics"!
He grasps this line, but he does not clear it out to find the new direction of poetry along this line.
Heidegger said that in asking what existence is, traditional metaphysics goes to the extent of forgetting existence itself. Its misunderstanding lies in the fact that it confuses existence with the one existing.

And Heidegger's misunderstanding lies in this: he falls into the same trap of a purely rational thinking about the world and entraps the world in the same conceptual net, isolating existence.

A poetic person is not a poetic "dweller" on the earth.

Heidegger dwells "poetically" in his "thoughts," but he thinks that "man dwells poetically on this earth." He follows Hölderlein's poetic aesthetics to express his philosophy.

Man's existential state on this earth does not have so-called "poetry."

Man suffers illness, suffering, poverty, hunger, plague, insects, beasts, floods, droughts, wars, storms, tsunamis, avalanches, explosions, volcanic eruptions, killings, earthquakes, thunder and lightning, falsehood, mudslides, racial prejudice, witchcraft, bias, jealousy, greed, tyranny, adultery, hate, fraud, being stabbed in the back, physical and spiritual usury, persecution, conspiracies, and brazen plots... These things follow us like a swarm of locusts covering the earth, surrounding us, covering us, swallowing us. This is the non-poetic environment of a poetic person! This is man's "non-poetic" existential state! "Poetry" only belongs to the realm of the human spirit. It is only the light of man's inner heart and the externalization of this inner light. But this "externalization" does not constitute an environment in which man "dwells." It is only a kind of spiritual transcendence by man over his sufferings on earth! A kind of spiritual dream state! A kind of dreamlike yearning and pursuit!

It does not constitute a "dwelling"!

Man's "original state" on this earth is not "dwelling."

Man is not a poetic "dweller" on this earth. Just as our planet drifts through the dark universe, so also man is a "drifter" on this drifting planet.

Dwellings, buildings, and thoughts have nothing to do with the essence of human existence or the state of human life.

According to the existential significance, "thought" is only the dregs of thinking, it is the waste product expelled by the spirit.

Thought is a conceptual construction; a construction is a non-conceptual thought. No matter how solid these two are, they cannot stand against the erosion of time, and they might collapse at any moment.

Man drifts on the earth in order to dwell. It is just drifting for no reason at all.

Such drifting is not peaceful, nor is it free; it is only drifting. **It is only the ceaseless moving of a spirit without a fixed dwelling.**

Man has no way to prevent a myriad of possible injuries and danger, and at any time he might fall into the trap of harm or danger without any way to prevent it.

Man is only "one who continues" and not "one who is fleeting." The "fleetingness" of individual life is just one link in the chain of limitless human continuity. Each chain is linked to another. Humanity is linked together one by one, and it never becomes disjointed by "fleetingness."

Nor is man a "saint" outside of himself.

He does not "possess" divinity, but he encompasses holiness, the heavens, and the earth in his body.

Man hears the call of himself; he does not hear the "divine" call of a "divinity" apart from himself. He replaces "god" by manifesting in "arrival" and by hiding in "departure."

Man is the one "arriving" and "departing," "manifesting" and "hiding," not "god."

Humans continue in "fleetingness." Life and death are to them the same as a kind of "continuation." Their existence never means "existence as existence"; just as their death never means "death as death." They do not "exist on this earth, under the heavens, and before god" because they exist or because they die. Their life and death are as "one."

Humans have no place to "dwell" upon the earth.

They can never "poetically dwell upon this earth" as Heidegger "**posited**." They cannot "make dwelling into a dwelling" because of "poetry"; nor can they "make dwelling into poetically dwelling, as dwelling is just dwelling, or make dwelling into non-poetically dwelling, as dwelling is not dwelling." This is because "dwelling" and "poetically dwelling" on this earth do not exist at all.

Heidegger merely "dwells" in his concepts.

Poetically and non-poetically do not construct human existence and non-existence; nor do these constitute absolute boundaries for distinguishing truth and non-truth.

Human existence has no "poetry" to speak of, even though existing humans are "poetic"; "poetry" is the continuation and engendering that humans have no hope of realizing. "Poetry" is the process of human hope.

Humans in the dark are just themselves.

Human darkness is also human light.

When humans arrive at "darkness," they also arrive at "light."

They cannot arrive at darkness or light apart from humans.

There is no darkness or light apart from humans.

Apart from humans, there is no one afraid of breaking "earth, heavens, saints, fleetingness," which are heaven, earth, man, and god, "the four dimensions which are essentially one."

These "four dimensions" only spring forth from "one" dimension in Heidegger's concept.

The world apart from the pollution of Heidegger's concept is

Pure and dimensionless.

In human existence "true existence" and "non-true existence" do not exist.

It is only existence.

When a wind blows past, it feels humans shaking.

Human existence does not have "poetry" as a special symbol.

It is only existence.

Humans do not need to go according to the arrangement of Heidegger's thought and "enter into" the earth, "enter into" existence.

Apart from human existence, humans who do not exist must "enter into" existence.

Humans are not only "a kind of existing ones" partially existing.

Humans **exist existentially**.

Humans **exist globally**.

Human construction without beginning or end is the beginning and end of all existence.

Humans prove the world's darkness.

They subdue and plunder themselves. They harm themselves in harming the heavens and the earth. They blaspheme and belittle themselves in blaspheming and belittling "holiness." They are "holy" because of themselves, and they are also "evil" because of themselves.

They monopolize themselves. They centralize authority and tyrannize themselves.

Humans are the despots of humanity.

Humans are the mixture of men, gods, devils, and beasts.

To humans, the misunderstanding of traditional metaphysics is not "mainly that it forgets existence," as Heidegger says. Rather, the key is that it forgets "humans"; it forgets **humans existing emotionally**! It forgets life's spiritual mystery, "the universal emotions of the human body"!

"Universal emotions" are related to the universe of the human body, and they are not related to thoughts and instruction. They are not related to logic, deduction, reasoning, and orderly conceptual forms apart from the spirit.

They are human nature before it was lost, and their properties have not yet been polluted.

Universal emotions are not a conceptual vector.

They are not sensory "feelings"; they are not visible and invisible qualities. They are themselves.

They disappear in language with local appearance.

They transcend the thoughts that cover them.

They are the unveiled self-view of life, insanely raging in "poetry."

Universal emotions are the source of "poetry."

They are the depths of the human body that were forgotten by philosophy.

The world is the experience of human depths.

Humans face danger. Humans themselves are dangerous. As they are crowded in this world of sufferings and joys, life and death, love and hate, they call for salvation with poetry.

"Poetry" is apart from existential poetry and poetic existence!

It is apart from existential art and artistic existence;

It is apart from existential aesthetics and aesthetic existence.

"Poetry" is apart from Heidegger.

Poets first discover and reveal "poetry," and in life's hidden, secret "universal emotions," they discover and reveal the tracks upon which it moves. Universal emotions distance themselves and come near in the universe of the human body.

Only the poet is their unique sensitive messenger; and they use poetry to wordlessly deliver and transmit them.

There is nothing poetic that allows men to poetically "dwell here" on the earth. Listening to the poetry in stillness is to listen to the stillness of universal emotions.

UNDERSTANDING THE DEPTHS OF THE HUMAN BODY: UNIVERSAL EMOTIONS
--Modern "Poetics" IV

What are "universal emotions"?
Where are "universal emotions"?
The only answer is to raise one's hand and smash the "conceptual pot."
Rescue the lost "philosophical master" out of the "pot"; rescue "philosophy" that is on the brink of suffocation.

In universal emotions, nothing is individual, independent, or closing itself off.
Planets are "planets" in mutual existence with other planets. They rotate in the same circle. This planet circumscribes the orbit of that planet.
A stick of incense burns, and the earth shakes. The ash of the incense is like an avalanche.
The sun and shadows move. The human palm covers the solar system. Heavenly bodies are hidden in the moving lines of the palm.
The breeze shaking the leaves sounds crisp. Hailstones strike at stillness. Sunlight shatters rubble. All these are "universal emotions" that are not yet covered; all these are constantly manifested; all these are the absolute affirmations of self that directly transcend "knowledge" and "concepts."

A voice sighing quietly and a wrinkle twitching on a face are like fuses, instantly igniting universal emotions at the heights of life experiences.

The human body closely and sensitively touches the nerves of the universe. They are in the most ordinary things that you contact every day.

They appear there, but you "are used to them," and you ignore them.

Any object contains the juncture where you can accidentally touch "universal emotions."

The whitecaps in a drop of water billow up to the heavens.

An eyelash reaches out and touches the mysterious line that communicates with the universe.

"Universal emotions" are the original face of the opening of the cave of life, which you have not yet touched.

They never reflect turbid sewage into the mood of your daily experience.

It is the "original face" that transcends time and space.

It is the same face of heaven and hell on the brink of catastrophe.

The universal emotions of the spirit are seamlessly one with all things; they cannot be separated. But they are also the forbidden place, which is difficult to approach, lying behind the metal wall of concepts.

They are the universe that we frequently watch, and we do not recognize their footprints when we see them.

Concepts are like a metal wall.
Poetry is a beam of penetrating polar light, which fiercely strikes towards the heavens, in an instant, with concentrated life.
At this time, the human body is like the collapse of the heavens. The spots of light are like a waterfall. They dazzle our eyes with their sparkles. Their shining breaks open the original heaven and earth of life.
Instantly, the flames are extinguished, and life hides itself again in darkness.
Universal emotions are the human body's experiences of the depths of the universe.

They lie concealed in the darkness like owls, but they do not "meditate" on the darkness.

They open and close their eyes, perch and fly, opening and closing their wings with complete spontaneity.
They are the shining mystery that opens up spiritual darkness.
Universal emotions "project" the universe of flesh and blood in the human body.
On the screen of life, they do not give up anything, nor do they add anything.
We can only sense the ruffling of their abundant feathers in our spirit, where we have insight into their small "righteousness."
Universal emotions are not the usual state of "authenticity" found in the quiet, direct life of Zen.
They are the "poetical inductions" that touch life instantly.
They are living, but they are not purely of "life." They are

true, but they are not purely "authentic." They are the review of spiritual experiences, which cannot be grasped in one's hand. They are the "entire scenery of the spirit," which is filmed from a distance and directly replayed through the lens of poetry.

They are not the peace of "self-closure," undisturbed in a purely Zen state; rather, they are the fetal movements of the entire universe, of an individual life.

They are not speculation, regardless if it is the speculation of rationalism or the speculation of mysticism. They are not a definite state of life. They are the thunder of spiritual solitude. They are the original face of "poetry."

Universal emotions are "poetic," not "Zen."
They are psychological and not concrete. They are not the rational constructs of advanced metaphysics. They are not "emptiness" with nothing in it. Nor are they the Zen-like "purity, directness, and practicality" of the real tendencies of human life. Rather, they are the poetic, inductive whole-body spiritual movements of the human body. "Universal emotions" are not a mysterious book of "philosophy."
They are "poetry" that is not religious, not philosophical, and not poetic.
They melt the boundaries between religion, philosophy, and poetry. They are the highest poetic "affirmation," which transcends affirmation and negation.

They are the "universal religion" that transcends religion. They are the universal poetry that transcends philosophy and poetry.
Do not ask what they are. Do not ask where they are. Asking and answering are superfluous.

There is only "poetry," erasing the darkness, extinguishing emptiness, indefinable. And yet it radiates unlimited, self-defining light from many sources.
Universal emotions cannot be defined with "is" and "is not." Nor can their position be described with "here" and "there." They are simultaneously behind you and before you. And regardless if they are in front or behind, they simultaneously point directly to your center.
Universal emotions have no center.
They tower simultaneously in all directions. You stand right on them in the middle of the place with no directions.
Do not try to think about them; they disintegrate in all thoughts, without a trace. They are not lost in "forgetting." They are not gained in "remembering." In not forgetting and not remembering, there is no gain or loss. When we attempt to set aside the forms of thought and limitations of language, such as "it is it," "it is not not-it," and "not not-it," then "universal emotions" appear naked on top of all existence. "Universal emotions" do not tie themselves to universal emotions. Universal emotions include "not universal emotions." We can only discover and grasp them in the poetic tendencies, which have never been brought to human

attention and which transcend their superficial "preposterous" appearances, bringing them up to the "absoluteness" of poetry. Thus, we find the misty path to the universe, which life has not yet dug.

Only when "universal emotions" are peeled away from the concept of universal emotions, can they manifest their actual "poetic" appearance.
Humans and the world are not two sides of one mirror; rather they are the same reflective side with no "crack" in the middle to hide the filth of concepts. Humans and the world shine on one another; they do not reflect each other.
The human lens is just the lens of the world.
It is the spotless, spiritual, poetic state.
"Universal emotions" are the "third eye" of humanity.
That is the eye that according to legend originally grew at the gateway to the human brain. It is the "heavenly eye" of humanity.
"Universal emotions" are the "third riverbank" of life.
There, the spirit of humanity finally feels as if it stands on solid ground.
The "third eye" is apart from human senses.
The "third riverbank" is apart from human general knowledge.
They are the great silence that chatters unceasingly. They are the "great reality" that escapes from the tyrannical imprisonment of concepts. Motionless freedom vibrates in "poetry."
"Universal emotions" have a great freedom that transcends structure.

It is not "original" structure; it is not "changing" structure; it is not "constructing" structure; it is not "deconstructing" structure. There is only the great freedom of "universal emotions" without "structure."

Life exists "artistically," not logically.

Humanity's highest spiritual expression is "poetry."

The realm of such "poetry" cannot be attained to by poets in just the pure significance of the word.

From "poetry" we can peek at "universal emotions."

But poetry is the "edge" and not the "source"; it can only evince the flow of life, but it is not the flow itself.

"Universal emotions" are not attached to "poetry," nor are they attached to "not poetry." They roar like stones and are as silent as thunder. They are a noisy, chaotic stillness and an un-restful, empty rim.

They are the whirlpool outside of a whirlpool; they are un-turning, rotating darkness. Not even light can escape from the depths of "all the experiences of the human body."

Universal emotions are a widespread net that is not reeled in. The "fish" that jump out of the net are still in the net that is hidden in the water.

Rational eyes look at them without seeing. Rational ears listen without hearing to this vast deep gong that "is hit without ringing, and rings without being hit."

Only "poetry" "strikes" at their gong and "contacts" the source of their electricity.

Universal emotions cannot be avoided. No matter how you dodge them, they are always opposing you face-to-face. At any time, they can hit you head-on. It does not matter if you open or close your eyes; it does not matter what direction you face; they are always your own eyes looking at you. They are your own life, which you cannot escape or avoid.

"Universal emotions" fill up the cup of life. You are what has been filled up. "Universal emotions" sparkle and dance with heavenly starlight in the darkness of the human body. It is your essence and blood that sparkle and dance unceasingly. It is the closely laid network of your cells. It is the frequency and rhythm of your blood-and-flesh body itself.

The spirit of modern humans is like a conceptual pocket, crammed full of fragments of conceptual things, blocking the connection between the human body and the universe.

Poetry is like a cleaning solution, clearing away the narrowness of rationality, washing out the filth of spiritual concepts to recover the purity that exists in not saying a word.

The universal language is like calm water with a deep current. A small grain of sand "does not speak" like the depths.

TRANSLATING SILENCE
—Modern "Poetics" V

This is a moment that has leaped out of simple honesty, a dead moment that seems to rampage. You hear the thunderclaps, the silent thunderclaps.
This is the first time in your life that you hear thunderclaps. It seems to come from the high empty space of the crown of your head; it comes from the end of the pitch black river of your arms; it comes from the distant place where your feet are standing or the empty edges of the blurry thickets and mountain shadows of your body, mute and silent.

You shower in the silence.
Your entire body listens to silence.
Yes, you have previously faced thunderclaps thousands of times, but you ignored the thunderclaps. You listened to them without hearing. It is only in this moment that you really hear the voice of the thunderclap. This is the silence of the spreading thunder of the human body. This is the stentorian silence of the entire universe at the moment of the dawning of life. It is a silence, rent by the collapse of the vast, boundless sky. This noise is too great, but your clogged body cannot hear it.

It has existed since the beginning, but you are so accustomed to seeing it that you do not notice it.

This is the sound that shocks the universe of the human body without speaking.
All languages thunderously crumble in this voiceless silence.
This is the vast, original language of the universe.
Human hearing must pierce through all other voices to hear it. This is the hidden, un-manifested silent thunderclap. It threatens you, and you are never able to defend against it. You cannot avoid it, but you constantly ignore its ceaseless, non-existing existence.
We humans constantly exist in the terror of its silence, an awesome silence that can kill us at any time in universal emotions. It is not sound; it is not the periodic vibration of sound waves. All sounds come from the original sound of this voiceless silence. All sounds are the echo of the silence of universal emotions. It is the non-speaking of the universal silence. We humans are placed in this constantly roaring silence from beginning to end, but we have never learned to hear or communicate the universal silence that is always in our ears.
We are only chattering sparrows in the universal silence, chattering outside of the rhythm of that great silence.
We are the expression of all communication, debate, explanation, teaching, acting, reporting, and all kinds of conceptual systems, all kinds of exchanged linguistic messages, which appear to be extremely illusory in the silent voice of universal emotions.

We humans live in such unreality.

Human existence is an illusion.
And in this same moment, in the unclear moment when life dawns, you see, for the first time in your life, the light of a thunderclap. It is the light of lightning that you have never seen before. It is the pitch black lightning that illuminates the heavens and the earth.
It is always there shining, but you look at it without seeing.
It is not a wave of light, it is not brightness, nor is it the contact between negative and positive electrical poles; rather it is darkness. It is the silent light that comes from the dark of darkness.
It is the same "light" as light.
Light is darkness seen by our physical eyes; darkness is the silent light that we look at without seeing.
This is such a marvelous momentary feeling; it is a feeling that transcends the feelings of the biological universe.
The utter end of light is darkness.
The source of darkness is light.
Light and darkness become one; day and night become one; the heavens and the earth become one; humans and the universe become one.
Humans exist universally.
Apart from humans, the universe becomes perishable.
Humans are a multidimensional existence.
Human existence is multidimensional and dimensionless.
You expose yourself to the moment when life momentarily dawns. This is a momentary moment that unceasingly and inadvertently slips away. It is a moment filled with eternity.

It is a dawning in your life. It is the first dawn of human existence. It is the simultaneous dawning moment of human thought and language.

You discover that all your life you have been dwelling in existential night, and you did not know it was night.

In the silence of dawn, you hear silence; in the darkness of dawn, you hear darkness; in the dawn of the human body, you hear the human body.

Just for this moment, you seem to have exchanged eyes and ears. You have gotten a supersensory sense of hearing and a supersensory sense of sight. They are the hearing and sight of the universe of the human body. They are the ears and eyes of the biological universe.

You discover that the sky above your head is not just an expanse of plain blue.

It deeply hides the universal silent voice that we listen to without hearing and the universal silent light that we look at without seeing.

It deeply hides the silence covered in "silence" that we are called to hear and the darkness covered in "darkness" that we are called to see.

It deeply hides the heavenly scenery that we have not yet discovered, as it is covered up in the "sky."

When we use the universal human body to view the sky, we receive a kind of thought from the universal human body. The sky is not the original sky. The familiar sky, which we have looked at for our entire lives without seeing, becomes something strange. It is no longer an idea of certain birds and clouds and blueness; it is no longer the beautiful memories of sunrises, sunsets, morning and evening clouds, and thunder and lightning; it is no longer the order and system to which you are accustomed; it is no longer an astronomical image that people can observe and draw.

At this moment, in the sky there is something that has previously been hidden from you, or something that you have seen every day and is so familiar that you exclude it from your sight. Did you forget the sky or did the sky place you into eternal forgetfulness? You discover that you were abandoned long ago. You discover that you never before discovered the simple meaning of the universe, which melts together and manifests all things, and at this moment you are in the place of universally existing.
You are just a "birding" bird. You have lost the unique bird of the universe. You have never been a universally existing bird. You placed yourself into the cage of "thought"; you drew together the imagination and freedom of "poetry."
At this time, the earth becomes strange to you.
The earth never returns to the old earth. The earth is apart from the earth. It is apart from the stones, forests, and rivers. It has never "earthily" earthed. In just one instant, it suddenly collapses in its "significance," "definition," "explanation," and polished thoughts. It is clear and also blurry. It is no longer a planet composed of rocks, tree roots, soil, ores, and the fossils of ancient living things. It no longer sketches out to us on paper that which is hidden, nor does it express

or reveal to us anything in symbols. Rivers are no longer the imprint of water; trees are no longer the green scars of wood.

You discover that the things upon which you firmly stood, the things which you called the "earth," are surprisingly the unreliable decks of a sampan, and at any moment you face the possibility of being drowned.

When you turn your gaze to look at yourself universally, you discover that you are no longer "human" in the old significance. You are shocked to see that your entire appearance is not. You are a stranger, and no one knows when you appeared on the earth. You are a foreign body in the universe that is blurry and unclear; no one knows whence you came, and you have no place to land.
In an instant, you sober up.
You heard the great, silent sound of the roaring thunder.
You finally broke through the silent, original language of the vast universe, which has been sealed and hidden for ages.
Direct silence, self-manifested silence, and digested silence.

March 20, 1992

The Origins of the Universe

"World, Your Exposed Body and Your Hidden Body"
Release Hysterically
February through April, 1987

THE "PRESENT" ABYSS

When you are petting a female animal or holding a woman, have you ever had the feeling, the sudden realization, that you are holding or petting an abstract thing?

It exists there, flooding out of your consciousness. You suddenly become confused about it.

This being that has taken shape as a woman or a female animal has something strange in her body: a cleft, an invisible opening. And when you see a fruit pit, a seed, a bird's egg, a cocoon, or a fish egg, you have the same feeling. When your eyes gaze on them limitlessly, they suddenly become gigantic.

It is as if there is an abyss hidden within them. And you suddenly fall into it.

And this is how a woman, a female animal, a seed, a bird's egg, or a fruit pit, a cocoon or a fish egg causes you to fall into the limitless, expansive opening of the universal black womb.

Symbols disappear.

This is an abyss "without anything" and "without nothing." Dark, mysterious, hidden stone clocks sound forth the hours of the universe. It ends its motionlessness and slowly begins to move in a circle. Here all living things become startled and freeze, annihilated yet at the same time impregnated by divine influence. The surging dinosaurs have blurry, shrublike faces; the rising and falling tigers are in chaos. All the visible things come pouring out of this invisible womb.

When you pull your eyes back, the world is still as it always was. The extrasensory abyss has returned to its hiding. But it is still "present." It takes form in all things. It takes form in the dark green rainwater, in the humid shadow of an ape; it takes shape as the earth, the zebras, leopards, and green peacocks. It reappears in the cruel beauty of the visible world.

Now the flooding consciousness is no longer a hidden cleft, an invisible opening. It has transformed its invisibility into visibility, and its nakedness can be seen in the forms of all things. It is in the secret place of a female animal in heat; in the broken egg-shell of a baby bird; in the split fruit pit and the sprouting seed; in the metamorphosis of an insect pupa or a fish egg…

It startles awake and drums to expose the muscles of the stones. It does not retreat, nor will it retreat. The background of the sky is still its deep blue aspiration.

The flood-like darkness has receded and coils behind its body like a giant python.

The elapsed time of eternity past recedes to both sides and stands still. And the earth unhurriedly appears wrapped in prehistoric wooly mammoths.

The water ripples on the invisible abyss. The roots grow and split open the invisible abyss.

The earth, tilted like a wide fan, opens its depths of depressed passions.

The earth's crust moves and stills. The hills and mountains break apart and solidify.

Like a carcass covered with congealed blood, the earth is calm in the deep red setting sun.

The copulating, pregnant living things relax in the original energy of desire...

The abyss shatters and cracks the faces of the huge stones; the ancient earth is rippled by blue-black desert winds and wrinkled by the grit of yellow sands.

The abyss can count millions of times when the wind eroded the boulders like bare bones; a time-elapse red cloud that disappears and reappears, licking repeatedly and crazily at its death.

But its eternal death is transcendent. Eternity is like a young, wild, native girl.
The sky is its beautiful, curvy waist.

It hangs soft quietness as arms of brown stones.

The black aperture opens its motherly desires towards the earth, and in space and time is eternally impregnated but never satisfied.

The abyss is the womb of the universe; thousands of stars move and turn inside it.

It surpasses our senses, yet exists within our senses, repeatedly hiding itself, repeatedly retiring from the world into all things. Circle upon circle of stone rotate and spiral in the earth with the shakings of the presence of the abyss.

March 27-28, 1987

ANCIENT FACULA

A facula, a bright spot, a leak. This is the earth in the darkness. It is considered a somewhat bright planet among the countless millions of stars and planets.

It is just a bright spot, a facula. Perhaps it is a facula that is aging. It might even be extinguished at any time.

It is as if the universe had a moth hole eaten away in it; a tiny little hole of light. But it is still shining there. This is a limitless, ever-spreading facula or hole of light. It contains rich miracles that throw mockery and offense to humanity.

In the boundless white darkness, there is always someplace that is sinking; there is always someplace that is protruding. This high-speed, ultra-rhythmic motion is invisible to the slow-moving human eye. If our vision could cross boundless time and space, we would see the beginnings and endings of the rise and fall of all the faculae. In the faculae we would see the earliest sinking of the oceans and protrusion of the mountains.

We would see the earliest bird take flight; we would see the earliest fish formed; we would see the earliest man stand upright; we would see the entire composition of the moving faculae in the countless varieties and complexities of life as they move up and appear.

This facula is so ancient. It is piled high with the old teeth of lengthy years.

The shaking day and the silting night draw the boundary lines and are melted into silent time.

As a human "I" only appear in human form within these boundaries; outside the boundaries, I am frightened like a beast and sprout branches and leaves. Man is a carrion eater. A burning corpse-candle of flesh and blood.

When it turns, it reverts to that great vulture with black-spotted feathers. Its image exposes the antiquity of downy, blood-drinking carrion and the dark night of beasts.

Oh look, humanity is so disoriented in the perplexing faculae: they walk beside a tree, but they cannot escape its ancient rings; they climb along a thick vine, but they can never climb to the end of the green sweeping its curves of deep meaning; they cross a black line of ants and discover that they are still standing outside the edge of the ant swarm; they climb onto a tall camel, but they can never get to the top of its hump.

There is always something stopping the human race. There is always something bothering humanity.

People trip and fall into the names of myriad items, even falling into a marvelous bird song that is hard to understand.

They are "trapped" in it and cannot find the exit from the bird's voice in its "bird song."

At the end of the boundless darkness, humanity sleeps in the same hole as an owl. They look at themselves with the angry, blood-dripping eyes of a horned lizard. They move backwards with the toads, using their back legs to scuttle into underground hidey-holes.

The fear of the king cobra is their fear, and they shrink into a coil around the earth and hide in the shadow of a hoof print.

Humanity is in a herd with the musk ox that are as rough as gravel, storing up billions of endurances before starting out in the fog of heaven and earth to complete its own carved statue.

The desolate, beautiful facula of the earth.

You see the brown mounds of dirt piling up on the frozen carcasses of musk oxen. The fence made of red bones greets the white sun on the heath.

The heron quiets the ice hills. The snow goose pulls apart the muddy rivers. The muskrat is the photographic negative of the white snow. The seal stops to lie on the pebbled beach. The emptiness of the evening overflows with brown and red flocks of birds. Two seals copulate in your miraculous feeling.

The ice fields on the two poles of the facula stand straight in the blue sky. The shadows look at each other. Lonely, they talk to each other.

It is as if we have finally passed through the long time of cold; now the heat is suddenly upon us. A thirsty herd of wild pigs and a herd of camels appear. A zebra sniffs out water hidden in the dirt.

After the short rain shower, the rainwater and the sun bloom with flowers.

The moon spins with the birds.

The evening bends its body to drink with the raised and lowered heads of beasts.

The facula of the earth stands up a little and then disappears in eternity.

A large grapefruit is hidden in the lonesome voice of the world. Now it suddenly pushes closer to the human race that looks at it without seeing; it is as an unknowable, silent green ball appearing for the first time.

March 18, 1987

THE VAST DARKNESS OF "DEATH"

The vast darkness of the human body is "death."

What we consider to be the "dark human body" of the universe is "death."

This is the undying darkness of death; the undeath of death's darkness. "Death" is itself and not itself.

"Death" has no direction in it, but it also has any direction. The direction of "death" lies between the compass points, and all of its directions are indefinite. "Death" is the "composite non-direction" of all the directions.

We never know whence death will spread out and come in or where death will spread out and go. It is as if it moves among the unintelligible things; it is as if it "halts" in the present moment.

"Death" is before death. It is before the time "without a time before it." It exists in the "non-existent" darkness. The predecessor of all things always retreats towards the next morning; from the moment it leaves it, it starts to move in the direction of recovering its oldest, original shape, the original shape of the life without life.

Death is the spreading darkness. Its "edge" still majestically rises and falls in its immense vastness.

"Death" bends darkness into itself. This vista of black darkness is its incomprehensibly mysterious self-image.

No "writing" can intelligibly describe "death"; no "spoken words" can deeply embody "death"; no "symbol" can overtly express "death." "Death" ablates everything into the darkness of its body. All darkness is expressed in "unnecessary expression."

"Death" stands against its own opposite, and it produces another opposite. All feelings and hopes of existence have the opposite meaning of "death." It is the undesired "desire." It is the sightless "sight." It is the unhearing "hearing." It is the "dead" root of vastness. It is the living reaction to "life."

It is the sightless broad view that covers up "sight."

It is the unhearing broad listening that stops up "hearing."

Silent "death" tumultuously sounds out darkness. It is the blurry, obscure background of the visible darkness.

It moves the profound blackness of the background. All visible things are independent of "death," and thus "are"; all visible things are blurred together in "death," and thus "are not." The "activities, lives and deaths, and existences," which are, together comprise the circle of "death" that "is no such circle." It is locked up within this circle and is also released outside the circle.

"Death" lies quietly within the "giant egg of darkness" that hatches it, just like the "breaking heavy and perfectly round non-egg" that is the egg of the universe.
It hides behind the pitch-black flood waters, and it surges up in those black floods.

It infiltrates bank after bank of clouds of stars, and it is reflected in the mysterious, inexplicable constellations.

Billions and billions of resonant, brassy and quiet, still suns "resonate and quiet" its "hidden body."

"Death" is behind death or "lying dormant" in the depths of the eternal "un-waking" darkness.

It is like the invisible grass seeds; the shadowless dust; the insensible, dormant insect eggs.

It is eternally exposed in its unexposed hiding place. In all the bright orbits and paths of the stars it hides its own dark path. When it shoots itself towards a cloud of pitch blackness, it immediately becomes its own "perplexing puzzle."

"Death," eternally offering itself to the great death!

"Death," eternally pouring itself out as libation to the eternal divinity!

Behold! How brilliant, how beautiful is "death" in the vast, deathless universe!

Oh, the burning day of disaster with the nova of the dying sun! The prominence of the sun's explosion is like a multi-colored shawl! The brightly-colored solar flares are like tassels made from feathers of light! The trembling, holy halo is a crown made up of solar winds and the sun's corona! The crazily singing, drunkenly dancing, spinning deathless "death" of the solar system and the Milky Way galaxy are a giant dark whirlpool...

Trillions of stars spin in a frenzy of delight around "death's" never-ending silence.

The death of a celestial body spreads out endlessly to the edge of the edgeless cloud of stars; it spreads out endlessly to the edge of the edgeless darkness. Red giant stars. Purple giant stars. Blue super-giant stars. The giant, distant star clock strikes the hours of the universe's divine annihilation. The rapidly receding, distancing cluster of giant stars sparkles like a school of grouper fish.

Silence tumultuously sounds out the darkness of death.

Dark "death" lifts high its herd of dark horse heads and rapidly retreats from the rolling darkness.

What a beautiful sacrifice of death! What a brilliant libation of death!

The mystery of the universe suddenly bursts open from "death."

It is like a seedless fruit.

March 23-25, 1987

"HUMANITY" IS FORMED IN THE ATTEMPTING

What is humanity? This is the doubtful question that all humans ask themselves.

Where is humanity? Humans are constantly searching for their place in the universe.

In order to determine themselves, humans drew a human "boundary" between themselves and everything else to distinguish the differences in nature and in position between humanity and everything else.

This boundary line is floating there; it appears between humans, animals, and plants. But as it is appearing, it is also sliding, and it disappears between humans and everything else.

Humans face the deepest levels of themselves; they come from the same place as everything else, and they are going to the same place. All things have the same origin, including the humans who doubt this discovery.

Humans are probably the long-extinct image of a hairy, ratlike, detestable animal. At their end, they erected a giant python shadow. They have the eyes of a badger; perhaps behind their eyes, the eyes of a badger lie in hiding. They never doubted that there is a "meaningless" meaning between lowly mice and exalted humans; perhaps it is the meaninglessness of distinguishing the "meaning" between these two things.

They get excited. Suffer. Dream. Their flesh spreads in all directions up to the edge of fantasy. But they are still self-confident, arrogant, and they call their activities on earth under the shining sun "creations": from a high-rise building to a poem. They are complacent and pleased with themselves. They glorify themselves boastfully with words like "great," "hero," "chief," "earth-shaker," and "pioneers of a new generation." They never realize that the pile of cultural "creations" from human history is so weighty! So heavy! They already cannot move it. These things just accumulate more and more thickly, and they pile up higher and higher, until they are so high that if all the cultural objects collapsed suddenly, they would bury humanity beneath them.

They are idiots. They are madmen. They are suffering from delusions. They have congenital depression … indistinct … desires … gushing out expressions, gushing out as maniacal laughter and crazy crying. Time and again these things climb along the cliff of "human" expression, but again and again they slide down the face of the cliffs on which they climb. Humans do not know why they are laughing, why they are crying. Nor do they understand the meaning of "laughter" or the meaning of "crying"! They try to transcend, to transcend that which cannot be transcended. They try to ascend, to ascend that which cannot be ascended. Their sufferings cannot cross over the boundaries of "humanity," regardless of whether this seemingly existent and non-existent "boundary" appears and disappears simultaneously between them and all things. The hours are brightly annihilated, pouring out like dry sand.

They are only laughing, crying babies, erecting for themselves "walls of expression." They are eternally formed as failed attempts within the snail's shell of the world.

Humanity's crazily ascending hopes are eternally extinguished in their own "human" name.

Humans have never taken off their "human" mask. Once humans take off their masks, they immediately see that they were never perfect; their complacent self-exultation, self-exaltation, and even their self-confidence are all tragic, absurd, and ridiculous. Humanity is only an unfinished "dream"; a kind of eternally unfinished attempt at "awakening."

Humanity! Humanity! What are you really? Where are you?

Do you hear the question of the voiceless voice? Do you know the answer of the voiceless voice? Perhaps there is no question and no answer; perhaps the question is the answer.

Humans takes themselves as the boundary to distinguish themselves from all the forms and objects in the world; but long ago, this "boundary" slipped and vanished from among humans, animals, and plants.

March 13, 1987

THE DARKNESS THAT ILLUMINATES ITSELF WITH A CANDLE

Crouch among the crouching beasts. Stand among the standing beasts. Leap among the leaping beasts. Lie among the lying beasts.

Appear among the moving beasts (including the human beast), but do not show yourself. Your body has the form of all beasts, yet is formless. It is unimaginable, illogical, unknowable.

It is the "existence" of self-existence, the "knowledge" of self-knowledge. It is the "secret self" of the world, the "hidden body" of the universe. Humans cannot discover it in the obscurity of the visible world.

Waking in the eyes of a lion, it opens up the black thorny, thicket.

Soundly sleeping in the body of a tiger, it is cloaked with fur, shocking red as the setting sun.

It exhibits quietness in the quietness of a deer; it leaks out clumsiness in the clumsiness of a bear, licking melting holes in the twilight of existence.
A bow and arrow are aimed against it. The broad daylight is pursuing it. But no sharp arrow can get close to it, and there is no daylight that can gnaw it away.

We lord it over our fearful selves without being afraid of anything.

Casting a shadow with fold upon fold of blood-spraying time, the quaking mud and dirt contains bedrock and metals in its depths.

It is the shape of every kind of beast, but it is not any one beast.

It is that giant beast from millions of years ago, and it is also the same giant beast from right now.

Its body exactly fits the critical physical form of a tiger or a panther. Its bearing is always smaller than or larger than the bearing of one's own body.

It is fitting and proper for one's self to distinguish between the roaring voices of that beast and this beast, but it is simultaneously this beast and that beast.

It is never larger than oneself, nor is it smaller than oneself.

It is always commensurate with the many different "volumes" of its own many different shapes.

This is the empty belly of the dark night. This is the startled, fleeing beast. This is the darkness that does not know where the darkness has gone. This is the darkness hiding in darkness. This is the darkness that cannot find its darkness.

This is the darkness that illuminates itself with a candle.

It wakes and sleeps in every moving animal.

It does not move in the "movement" of all the beasts.

The beasts, which are seeking food, copulating, living healthily, aging, appearing, and disappearing, vary in its invariability.

It is at that end of the world where all noises are silenced.

It is an unborn, undying bright and brilliant hazy obscurity.

It is the form that retreats from form.

It is light from the self-illuminating inky blackness.

The light of human imagination will never ever reach it.

March 10, 1987

THE RIDDLE OF ESSENCE

What is the strength that attacks and moves all the life in the world?

Does it exist in the world itself or does it exist outside of the world?

Does it exist in the "center" of the world, or is it "behind" the world?

Humans ask these questions over and over again in every generation.

Countless days have gradually given them all kinds of suppositions and guesses.

In Kant's heart this is the unknowable thing in itself.

Hegel speculates that it is an idea.

Schopenhauer came to understand it as the essence of blind will.

Nietzsche rediscovered it as the piercing light from the tragic spirit of the ancient Greeks that elevated and affirmed life; old Zhuangzi thought that it was the emptiness at the beginning of all matters and things...

But any "concept" is inadequate to explain it.

It is inexplicable, but always there.

Humanity gives birth and enters death for generations; the world of life moves in an eternally endless cycle. Each individual life is fleeting, temporary, limited; it is just a passing moment in the vast length of eternity. But life itself will never perish, and the entire world of life will never end.

Life is eternal. The tremendous "power" of the world of life is also eternal.

It is as if an invisible ray of life transmits across the universe.

The heart and spirit of humanity seem to receive the limitless message of this transmission over and over again.

Maybe it is the heart and spirit of humanity constantly receiving back its own message that it transmits out to the heavens.

Suddenly, we discover in the vast heavens the "naked dance of identity."

It has been transformed into the wheel of a giant, naked sun and a giant, naked bird.
That is pure light covering and reflecting a scene without humans. There the shadow of the giant bird dances with the

shadow of the giant sun; they have been revolving against each other for so long.

This female bird that symbolizes enlightenment always presents herself as a pure virgin in the original sacrifice! As the red sun crazily pursues her, she instantly spreads her desire-colored plumage towards his stark naked golden body in shameless feminine desire. In the peaceful quiet of the heavenly frustration that lost its mask she spreads open, and he unites with her!

He completely "opens" in exposure.

Pure and clear.

As the many-petaled dream of the world.

In that instant of simultaneous day and night, the female ostrich takes the virginity of the white sun a million times over.

The stark naked, golden body of the giant wheel of the sun!

Allowing the insatiable feminine desires to repeatedly ravage!

A million floods of rushing blood! A million jolts of electricity! A million times collapsing into one moment!

All the heavenly bodies are a vast expanse of uninhibited, dripping red light!

This is the motivating force leading to the impregnation and birth of the world!

During the prehistoric dancing shadows of the white sun and the ostrich, "sun sperm" is repeatedly shot into the female ostrich. The various images of the great cycle of life are eternally impregnating! Destroying! Creating! Resurrecting!

The universe revolves in an untraceable circle with a fishy smell.

A million days are as a moment.

The muscle of the world will never stop its turbulence. It is as ancient as palms, soles, paws. As bright green as foliage, eternally sprouting.

This is the extensive view of the universe.

Delicate and pretty. Empty and spiritual. Vast and deep.

It seems that we are suddenly just discovering it for the first time.
In reality, it has existed for billions and billions of years.

Although the visible world has passed through endless exchanges, which are hard to imagine, with countless individual lives appearing and disappearing, it continues to exist there. Never ending! Never stopping! Never perishing!

It has no beginning and no end.

It is the fleeting moments of eternity's past, present, and future.

It is not something we can logically analyze or prove, nor does it have Dionysian or Apollonian spiritual beauty in our ideal world!

It is more beguiling and shivering than anything else!

It is the clear abstruseness and agitated peace of the universe's life.

February 20, 1987 (first draft)
April 23, 1987 (revised version)

THE EMPTY CAVE OF THE "NON-EXISTENT" BODY

All dreams are not real; reality is just a dream. The "existence" of being is a dream, and the "non-existence" of being is also a dream. It is a huge whale-shaped dream that is not existent and not non-existent.

This dream body seems to open up to us as an eternally moist water cave with a boundlessly spreading opening.

The waves come continuously in clustered groups.
The fish and shrimp come continuously in clustered groups.
The people and beasts come continuously in clustered groups.

Life uses its countless "existent" physical forms to penetrate the boundless "non-existent" body.

Human vision bends the waves like the tongue of a reef licking and finding the bitterness. But human vision never discovers and never can discover the wave of shaking black rhythm within the water waves.

Both human ears hear the water's voice like the sound of a ball rolling on the earth, but they never hear that sounding darkness submerged within the depths of that ball of water.

It seems that within a moment's time, thousands of waves are suddenly touched and move. The water waves roil. The water spreads as it flows out of this whale-shaped dream body. They constantly approach humanity, but there is no time when humanity approaches them.

The bright green leaf veins spread out in a soft, flowing river.

Who can tell if it is really leaf veins or a river!

The ichthyosaur leaps into the air. The giant clam opens and shuts. Who knows why the leaping ichthyosaur leaps into the air? Or why the opening and shutting clam opens and shuts?

Blue-green algae and red coral appear, always thinking to express but never expressing bitter feelings.

The hazy sea lily reflects a handprint. Is this a handprint or a sea lily?

And humans cannot come close to a large tree, at least they cannot guess if the rings circling the heart of the tree are annual rings or the flowing memories of time?

Somewhere in the empty heart is an absolutely purified environment.

Here, there has never been a pair of feet to brush over it; there has never been a finger to suck. We suckle our fill from the original nipple that gathers and scatters all images and shapes, but we never suckle our way to the nipple's source. We bathe drunkenly in the constant, surging multifarious flow that nurses all things, but we can never bathe in any flow outside of this all-encompassing one.

It is as if there is a prehistoric fossil floating up on the water that is constantly showing us mysteries. But no one in the human race can explain the mystery; no one recognizes this mysterious "universal emblem."

Only wings can sip the clarity here.
Only hooves can explain the quietness here.

This whale-shaped, empty cave of the "non-existent" body opens the world, and in the continuous figures of "existence" it manifests the boundless truth and richness of "non-existence." But, this black cave of the whale body, which perplexes humanity and angrily swings the universe, is just a dream of a swinging ball of water "without a single drop of water."

March 12, 1987

THE MOTHER OF THE UNIVERSE

When we bring all our knowledge and our ability to imagine into the universe, we will feel as though we have suddenly fallen into limitations, and we are able to do nothing.
No matter what, we cannot grasp or understand this vast, limitless thing. Perhaps our destiny is to be unable to escape from a certain human bondage.

It seems that our mind leads us astray from the beginning.

Maybe that immense, endless, limitless, boundless, giant thing is not the nature of the universe (if it is possible for the universe to have a certain nature); that thing is not the most intrinsic, essence of the universe (if the universe has a certain intrinsic essence). It may not even be the universe itself.

It is just the present image of the universe.

The real material universe could never spread limitlessly like this into the expanse of space; nor could it ever be so far from us, be purely separated from us, or be apart from us physically. We do not need to use our "limitedness" to seek assurance of that "limitlessness." We just need to sense it from within ourselves, to discover it. We just need to understand it from any other limited, material thing that is beside us. It "exists" in the forms of time, space, the laws of cause and effect, etc. that we use to know it. But it is not any one limited, material, partial thing. It is complete within itself, self-fulfilling, and whole. We borrow forms to know it, but it escapes from every form. We use conceptual frameworks of time, space, and cause-effect relationships to contain it, but it exceeds the knowledge of all conceptual frameworks.

It is the dark thing which cannot be grasped and is limitless and boundless.

This is "Buddha"; it is not the "Eastern Buddha" in an apparent human form; it is not any kind of divine, honorable, limitless Buddhist religious symbol for "Buddha."

It is not any kind of animal, nor is it any kind of plant;
It is not a beast, as it does not have claws;
It is not a bird, as it does not have wings;
Nor is it a human, as it does not have any visible "limbs."

But it is not dead and quiet; rather, it is moving and alive. It does not appear in the life form of any animal or plant, but it is the mother of all life.

It is the shapeless darkness that is like a chrysalis, a giant black chrysalis.

It is not the near darkness, nor is it the far darkness. It is not this patch of darkness or that patch of darkness. It is merely the darkness without want, without color, and without lack.

We cannot know it, nor can we clearly fathom it. We cannot tell whence it came, and we do not know if there will come a moment when it will end.

It moves all things, but it remains frozen without moving itself. It does not live and does not die, but it soaks up both life and death.
It always kneads and wiggles in the unmoving darkness. It kneads and shapes the rivers and trees; in the dark, it releases the flying birds and the centipede with a hundred legs. It kneads and shapes a human-shaped "worm," first as a white lily; it allows this ever dissatisfied "beast-form" to have an existence of drinking wildly without getting drunk!

All movement of life and life that moves originate in it.

It is the universal darkness, and it transcends the darkness without beginning.

It sits cross-legged behind the white darkness.

It lives alone behind the rough earth and the stone cave of the quiet universe, behind the faces of the myriad beasts.

We only feel it in our hearts. As soon as we turn towards it and look, we discover a faceless "Buddha"—a chrysalis-shaped, giant "thing of darkness."

February 24. 1987

THE IMAGE OF THE "IMAGELESS" WORLD

Its body is limitless.
What it touches is not any physical body; rather, it touches the body of space itself.
It is forever small as a moment.
The closed human body falls through barrel hoops.
The shape does not become its shape.
A palm tree releases its own wings and is crazily rigid; the lidded view sees the silence of birds' eggs that want to be hidden and want to be manifest; the roots and vines of wild grass snakes manifest empty vastness.
An instant explodes into an eternity.
Blind imagelessness sees that which has no image.
Deaf silence hears silence.
Quiet the pulsating of the giant, wild heart. Sink into dreams like wine. The only one who can drink crazily without getting drunk is the eternal emptiness.

The heaven and earth are leaking from a deep, deep crack. The barren beasts are dark like faint red coals. The tree of darkness constantly sprouts twigs that angrily surge in sign language. The self enlightens its own darkness as brightly as a cave. The darkness discovers darkness without a place to hide.

The visible darkness cannot be seen in the dark.
The invisible darkness can be seen in the dark.

The bright flames of darkness expose the pitch-black hidden palm; the five fingers invisibly flow into and get lost in the perforated plate of darkness.

The never-ending sound of hands clapping silently covers the murky depths.
The palm is not a palm; neither is the non-palm a non-palm.
The shape of a palm is not the shape of a palm; neither is the shape of a non-palm the shape of a non-palm.
This palm grasps and holds but never obtains.
It is, but it does not exist.
Do you understand? The light is the visible darkness; death is another kind of existence.

No matter that the serpentine dance of explanation cannot be explained. It is emaciated and clumsy without an iota of percipience.

Is that which is suddenly extinguished lightning? A deer? Is the hidden shape of an ox the first light of dawn? A wild fire? The crisply audible sunlight is like porcelain beads; the claw marks of the mysterious eagle owl are like eyelashes when you blink; astonished, foolish stones dilate the pores of early morning.

Men and women stand motionless in their lust.
Pine trees open and embrace the emptiness.

All things in the universe are positioned in each other, boundless without any position. All things seep into each other, flowing and getting lost in the losing flow.

Thigh and thigh weep bitterly through the night until they are hoarse.

The hungry stones are like cattle, like leopards, pouncing in rage. Are cattle really cattle? Are leopards really leopards? That "view" deludes you; you are looking at the false, empty "view"!

In the horrified shape of split vision, all things are without shape! Fish in deep water sip imagination; birds high up in the sky chirp and split fire; black ants and red ants move in flows across the wrinkles of eternity's face; an eagle's feather gives vent to death's sinister glance.

Oh! Who is loudly shouting from within death like a dog's bark? Tsk! It is hard to endure the simplest logic.
Wine in the depths of the crock turns back into water.
A pearl inside the black of an oyster shell turns back into a grain of sand.
All things have neither this nor that. This and that are both nothing. Nothing, nothing.
Are you still standing there without moving? Why haven't you left the formless emptiness yet?

No one sees me. No one hears me. No one follows behind me. I am vertically alone. I step on my own shadow till it hurts. Yin and yang do not have pressure points. Movement and stillness have no door. The door without a door closes and opens.

Emptiness has no heart. The ending leaves no scar. A search only finds a pile of loneliness.

The unending death is eternally within "death." Ashes extinguish themselves without wind. Barriers crop up. The broken goes in the "exit"; the unbroken is in the "entrance." No exit and no entrance. The silent voice asks questions. The voiced silence has already answered. No question and no answer. As a question and as an answer.

Suddenly we hear a crocodile and the black monologue of an empty glass.

Shadows shake shadows.
Dust rolls up and takes away dust.
The absent dead do not go beyond the present living.
The absent otherworld does not divulge the present this-world.
The dream is relaxed by waking. Life is relaxed by death. Relaxation cannot be relaxed.
Laughter piggybacks on crying. Humans piggyback on ghosts. Backs piggyback on non-backs.
The boundless points of light are as dangerous as their danger; as small as their smallness.

If we cut open the veins that criss-cross and twist around the human body, we still cannot open up every twist and turn of the maze that is human life.

It is too mysterious to explain.

An infant's cry does not have a dying skeleton. The leopard's spots are like delirious ravings.

The body obstructs the portrait. The thunderbolt that shakes loose hair and nail clippings exhibits a raging emptiness.

The sitting deer with large antlers holding up the earth has four hooves like eyes.

The water snake swims like a crinkly shadow of a pole.

White hair snaps the withered vine in pieces.

A beast never threads its way out of the ring of its feet; a fish never swims out of the ripples in the pond; a bird never flies out of the startling barrier.

An empty reflection is fathomless. A trap surges crazily. The mournful howl of the wolf burns.

A circle of crazy laughter strangles time to wake it up.

The leisurely celestial phenomena are savagely fierce.

A swoon paints black nightmares.

March 17, 1987

ABOUT THE AUTHOR

Huang Xiang was born on December 26, 1941 in Guidong County, Hunan Province. His entire life has been spent in the pursuit of the freedom to live and the freedom to write. He was incarcerated a total of six times.

Huang Xiang began publishing his work in 1958, and his poetry was selected for the 1958 National Poetry Anthology in China. He was also the youngest member of the Guizhou chapter of the China Writers' Association. In 1959, he was stripped of his membership due to political persecution, and publication of his works has been banned ever since, for more than 40 years now. Over the long course of his intellectual life, Huang Xiang has continued steadfastly in the undercurrents of the underground writers' movement, never ceasing to rebel in the battle of the pen. His writings cover many genres, including poems, poetics, literary theory, poetic philosophy, semi-autobiographical novels, essays, notes, political treatises, and memoirs. Over the decades, Huang Xiang's work has passed through the checks and searches of numerous political campaigns, and now, fortunately, more than 3 million words of it remain.

From 1978-1979, Huang Xiang began the enlightened democracy movement in China by establishing "The Enlightenment Society" and launching the literary journal *Enlightenment,* both the first to be unaffiliated with the Communist Party government. These were preludes to China's modern Democracy Wall Movement and to the modern poetry movement. At the same time, Huang Xiang criticized Mao Zedong, denouncing the Cultural Revolution and raising the matter of human rights for the Chinese people under a totalitarian system.

After *Enlightenment,* Huang Xiang continued to participate in the democracy movement with the creation of several mainland Chinese popular publications, such as *The Rising Generation* and *The Celestial Constellations of Chinese Poetry.* He also became one of the principle editors of the Bejing Yuanming Garden Artist Colony's civilian publication *Great Commotion.*

Recently, a number of famous scholars have broken through the ideological chains of the government and now have begun to revise the prior hostility towards Huang Xiang with respect to his literary and historical contributions. His free-verse poems, which he began writing as early as the 1960s, were selected for inclusion in *Looking Back on Trends in Modern Poetry—Misty Poets Volume* (Beijing Normal University Press), *One Hundred Years of Chinese Literary Classics* (Beijing University Press), *Anthology of 20th Century Chinese Literary Classics* (Haitian Publishing Company), *Course on the History of Modern Chinese Literature* (Fudan University Press), *One Hundred Selections from 20th Century Literature* (Xueling Publishing), and *Free-verse Poetry* (Workers Press). However, his own books still cannot be published openly in China today. These books include a poetry anthology entitled *Huang Xiang—a Drinking Beast who is not Drunk,* a collection of literary theory *Open Wounds,* poetic philosophy *The Thunder of Deep Thought,* a semi-autobiographical novel *The History of Spirit and Flesh—an individual under the sky and the individual's sky,* essays and jottings *Jottings from the Pittsburgh Dream Nest*, an autobiographical documentary *Hustle and Loneliness—The Autobiography of Huang Xiang and the Splendid Kernel of the Far East*, as well as political treatises and memoirs.

In 1993, Huang Xiang was invited to the United States for the first time, and in that same year he was awarded the International Human Rights Watch Freedom of Speech Writers' Award. In 1997, Huang Xiang was invited to the United States again, where he now resides with his wife Qiu Xiao Yu-Lan.

Huang Xiang is modern mainland China's first free poet and writer, and his writings are the most prolific. Because he has been banned for most of his life, Huang Xiang's writings are relatively unknown both in China and throughout the world. They began to be discovered at the end of the last century and the beginning of this century, with the publication in New York, Hong Kong, and Taiwan of a poetry anthology *Huang Xiang—a Drinking Beast who is not Drunk*, a collection of poems *A Selection of Huang Xiang's Banned Poetry* and a collection of essays *Jottings from the Pittsburgh Dream Nest,* and *A Lifetime is a Promise to Keep.*

The three volumes comprising *House of the Sun Notebooks* (*Always Lonely*, *The Thunder of Deep Thought,* and *Open Wounds*) were published in Taiwan, and they include the first publication of the author's poetics, literary theory, and poetic philosophy.

Sampsonia Way Publishing

Sampsonia Way is the publishing arm of City of Asylum. It's a home for the work of exiled and endangered writers around the world; it publishes banned books in translation and anthologies of contemporary writing from countries where free speech is under threat, and it serves a global community of readers and writers through the online literary journal, SampsoniaWay.org.

City of Asylum

City of Asylum provides long-term sanctuary to endangered literary writers, along with a broad range of residencies and programs in a community setting to encourage cross-cultural exchange. We also anchor neighborhood economic development by transforming blighted properties into homes for our literary-based programs, energizing public spaces through public art with text-based components.

City of Asylum is a 501(c)(3) nonprofit. To learn more about us and our programs, please visit our website: cityofasylumpittsburgh.org.

ALSO BY SAMPSONIA WAY

The Conspiracy, a novel by Israel Centeno

"His fleshy, psychologically penetrating work is one of the great undiscovered literary experiences of Latin America."
—Aurelio Major, Co-founding editor of *Granta en Español*

Generation Zero: An Anthology of New Cuban Fiction
Edited by Orlando Luis Pardo Lazo

"In Generation Zero, sarcasm, deterritorialization, transvestism, fragmentation, colloquialism, hybridization, adventure and imagination are redesigning Cuban identity, recovering their power of subversion and resignifying Utopia."
—Paulo Antonio Paranaguá, *Le Monde*